To John Christmas 1982

Love [illegible]

[illegible], Diane, Tony

& John.

Famous Sporting Fiascos

BY THE SAME AUTHOR

Great Commercial Disasters

Amazing Times!

Famous Sporting Fiascos

STEPHEN WINKWORTH

Illustrated by Jaques

BH

THE BODLEY HEAD

LONDON SYDNEY

TORONTO

British Library Cataloguing
in Publication Data
Winkworth, Stephen
Famous sporting fiascos.
1. Sports – Anecdotes, facetiae, satire etc.
I. Title
796 GV191
ISBN 0–370–30450–0

Printed in Great Britain for
The Bodley Head Ltd
9 Bow Street, London WC2E 7AL
by Redwood Burn Ltd
Trowbridge, Wiltshire
Set in Linotron Palatino
First published 1982

CONTENTS

WHAT ARE SPORTING FIASCOS?

When sport was first invented it was all about winning. This concept was updated by the Bishop of Pennsylvania, preaching in St Paul's Cathedral in 1908 on the occasion of the London Olympic Games. 'The important thing,' he pronounced, 'is not so much to have been victorious as to have taken part.' The sentiment was echoed a few days later by Baron de Coubertin, the founder of the modern Olympic movement.

Any fool can see that all this is pure hokum. The only purpose of sport has always been to show that you can do whatever it is better than the next man or woman. If you try to play worse than other people it may be good for your soul, but it doesn't do much for the game. Winning is what it is all about. (There used to be an old-fashioned self-indulgent notion that sport was supposed to be fun, but now we know better. Either you are a supporter, with a manic light in your eye and a heavy weapon in your hand, or you are a player, a mere cog in a vast money machine, who has about as much hope of enjoying the action as a soldier on a battlefield.)

This was roughly my view of sport until I heard of the fisherman on the River Warche. This fisherman was one of a group of campers who pitched their tents one August afternoon in 1972 on the banks of this picturesque Ardennes stream in southern Belgium. Let us linger for a moment and visualize the scene: the mossy old weir, the grassy banks, the wooded hills... One can imagine the confident gleam in the fisherman's eye as he pulled on his waders and set off for the long reeds by the river's edge. How peaceful, how Arcadian sport can be!

Before long he was back with his catch: four unexploded handgrenades and three smoke bombs (and not a fish in sight). Luckily none of them went off, but to be on the safe side the campers called in the bomb-disposal experts, who fished fourteen more Second World War handgrenades out of the river. The campers packed up their tents and moved on rather hastily. They had not, after all, come to the Ardennes to witness a replay of the Battle of the Bulge.

Although this story failed to dispel my view that sport is at times liable to take on military overtones, it did give me my first hint that there might be a new approach to the subject, for that Belgian's afternoon of fishing was a straight action replay of the original sporting fiasco. That original fiasco happened many centuries ago to a fisherman in the Bay of Naples and had, I am thankful to say, nothing whatever to do with war – which is not in any case something the Italians are very good at (though their talent for military fiascos is unparalleled).

The Bay of Naples used to be a marvellous place for fishing, despite its traditionally being used as the town's chief rubbish dump. One evening a fisherman was lazily trolling his line on the *'lastra d'argento'*, as the song calls it, when he felt a pull and quickly hauled it in – to find hooked on the end not a fish but one of those Italian wine bottles in a straw basket – a *fiasco*. These *fiaschi*, or flasks, have a habit of floating about just under the surface, and their straw handles are guaranteed to snare any fishhooks that come within range. So, every time a fisherman hauled up something that was not a fish it came to be referred to as a *'fiasco'*, and eventually the word found its way into the English language to mean any kind of unexpected, foolish or disastrous happening.

If there are fiascos in fishing, I reasoned, they must exist in other sports as well. Before long I heard of the boxer at the Munich Olympics whose gumshield fell out in the middle of a fight. It's not particularly easy picking up a small object off a canvas floor while wearing boxing gloves, and as he scrabbled around frantically on his hands and knees the referee counted him out. His Olympic hopes were ended. This, I immediately recognized, constituted another sporting fiasco.

Then I heard about the cricket team on tour in the South Pacific who went out for a spot of practice just after a heavy rainstorm in Fiji. Apparently at certain times of the year in Fiji after the rains there is a species of frog which pops out of holes in the turf to mate. The cricket pitch was as full of holes as a Gruyère cheese, and there were so many frogs around that the players kept stepping on them. The practice session had to be abandoned – it is not very nice trying to play cricket on top of a slippery layer of squashed frog.

The next one I heard of was the British kayak pair in the slalom event at Augsburg in the 1972 Olympic Games who got stuck upside down in the rapids, wedged against a rock – all you could see was the bottom of the kayak, and no sign of life. A BBC commentator remarked: 'I don't wish to appear pessimistic but I sense our medal chances are slipping away.' Later it turned out that one of the pair had lost his watch during the experience and the entire slalom course – an artificial structure rather like a vastly magnified rock-garden waterfall, with water pumped through it at thousands of gallons a second – had to be turned off and emptied while they searched for it.

By this time I had become convinced that there was a whole area of sport which hitherto had not received the attention it deserved. What redeems sport from being merely a brutish contest for supremacy, or a cynical branch of big business, I suddenly realized, is its irrepressible tendency to go unexpectedly and delightfully off the rails. Someone's trousers explode or a golfer is confronted by a burning bush, or a bat gets in among a lot of ice hockey players. A fiasco is a deeply moving experience, really, and often in quite unexpected ways – as yachtsman J. R. Williams found out one peaceful day in the summer of 1974 while sailing in the Menai Straits. His spinnaker was up and he was gliding effortlessly before the wind, admiring the scenery. Gazing at the nearby Belan Fort he could see a group of figures on the battlements. The women were brightly dressed, and bottles and glasses were visible. Suddenly there was a tremendous explosion and smoke filled the sky. The boat rocked alarmingly and Williams peered up to see if his mast was still intact. When he hauled down the fluttering spinnaker he found five holes near the top. They were made, it transpired, by a cannonball, negligently set off from one of the fort's medieval cannons by some bright spark in Lord Newborough's party. A little incident like this epitomizes how carefree and yet stimulating sport can be. It must have made a deep impression on Mr Williams at the time.

There is a fiasco somewhere within every sporting event. Assuming that it is a competitive sport, there must be a loser and a winner (a tie is a sort of fiasco too, though a poor one). For the winner there is immediate satisfaction. But the loser's reward is more lasting: to have committed the fiasco of losing. To have been responsible for a fiasco – provided one has not done it intentionally – is sport's greatest reward.

I gathered the fiascos in this book from many sources. In all cases I have tried to convey as faithfully as possible the critical facts of the historical event as it occurred. But I am aware that this is just the beginning – that this work is merely the first brick in the temple. I hope for all its shortcomings and omissions it will encourage others to devote themselves wholeheartedly to the collection and study of sporting fiascos; because if there is anything more satisfying than experiencing a fiasco oneself, it is the knowledge that someone somewhere has just been involved in an even bigger one.

Stephen Winkworth

1

Trying Too Hard

One way you can be sure to cause a fiasco in sport is by trying too hard.

THE HITCH-HIKER'S GUIDE TO THE MARATHON

The 'Marathon' commemorates the heroic activities of Pheidippides in 490 BC. History often fails to relate, however, that for at least part of the distance the dashing Greek hitched a lift on a goat. Inspired, no doubt, by this precedent, many modern marathon runners have also availed themselves of alternative means of transport. They shall all remain nameless here, except for two.

Dimitries Velokas finished third in the Athens marathon of 10th April 1896, behind the winner Spyros Louis and the second-place C. Vassilakos. But Velokas was ignominiously stripped of the blue and white singlet of Greece when G. Kellner, who had finished fourth, protested that he had seen Velokas alighting from a carriage a short distance from the end. The carriage was, of course, a symbolic replacement for the goat, but it is the outraged Kellner who appears in the official record books as third man.

It must have been doubly distressing for Velokas to see the winner Louis, far from dropping dead after the race as precedent demanded, happily accepting a shower of gifts from all directions, including a voucher for a year's supply of free meals, shoe-polishing for life, and the freehold of a large field, later named the 'field of Marathon'. Only the fact that he was already married prevented him from accepting the hand of the daughter of a local millionaire. (All these gifts were, of course, out of keeping with the amateur spirit of the Olympic Games, and Louis never ran again.)

Overcome with heat exhaustion during the Stockholm marathon of 1912, Shizo Kanakuri was tottering past a villa on the outskirts of Tureberg when he noticed people in the garden with tall glasses of orange squash in their hands. Kanakuri begged a sip, then a glass, then another glass – and ended up taking the train back to Stockholm. But shame overcame him and he did not, like some others, rejoin the runners; instead he spent a night in a hotel, then slipped away without telling anyone what had happened and took the first boat back to Japan. His disappearance was a mystery at the time.

In 1962 a Swedish journalist tracked him down in Tamana in southern Japan, and Kanakuri decided to travel back to Sweden and finish the race, revisiting the villa where he had stopped. A tardy marathon (fifty-four years, eight months, six days, eight hours, thirty-two minutes and 20.3 seconds to be precise), but as Kanakuri pointed out, he had acquired en route a wife, six children and ten grandchildren, all of which takes time.

MESSING ABOUT ON THE RIVER

Anyone with an interest in rowing will have noticed that there is a boat known as an eight, which contains nine men – eight of them facing backwards and rowing, the ninth facing forwards and steering – and another known as a coxless four, in which four men face backwards: none of them can see where they are going, but all are united in the common belief that it is in the right direction.

The origin of the coxless four lies in a curious incident which took place at Henley Regatta in 1868.

The previous year at the Paris Regatta four extraordinary oarsmen from New Brunswick in leather braces and a clumsy-looking boat had defeated all the opposition. The boat had no cox and was steered by bow, partly with his oar and partly with an ingenious contrivance attached to his feet. This gadget caught the fancy of W. B. Woodgate of Brasenose College, Oxford, a spirited and innovative young oarsman with a keen eye on the main chance.

For the Henley Stewards' Challenge Cup of 1868 Woodgate announced that Brasenose would enter a coxless four; he himself would steer at No. 3 with a wire and lever attached to his stretcher. W. Wightman Wood of University College quickly protested that this was against the rules and the stewards declared that Brasenose would be disqualified if they did not carry the customary cox, even though the rule book in fact said nothing on the subject.

Woodgate was not to be put off by this. He enlisted the support of a remarkably daring Brasenose man, F. Weatherly, and at the start of the race the Brasenose boat contained the usual five men: Weatherly, recruited as cox, then Champneys, Rumsey, Woodgate at No. 3 and Crofts. The umpire gave the signal for the 'off' – and Weatherly plunged straight into the Thames, leaving the other four to row on without him.

Brasenose won by a hundred yards – and were immediately disqualified.

Back at the start Weatherly struck out for the riverbank, but became entangled in some siren waterlilies and only just made it. It is lucky that he did. He survived to become a songwriter and gave the world 'Danny Boy'.

GOLD FOILED

During the 1976 Olympic Games in Montreal Sergeant Jim Fox, fencing against the Russian 1972 Olympic silver medallist and 'Merited Master of Sport' Boris Onishenko, noticed that the electronic scoring system was registering 'hits' which Fox knew for certain were not being made. The foil was examined by Carl Schwende, 'Chief of Discipline', who stated that the weapon had been tampered with: it had been wired in such a way that a winning hit could be scored by pressing a button in the handle, without having to make contact with the opposing fencer.

The news electrified the Games. Colonel Willie Grut, Secretary General of the International Union of Modern Pentathlon and Biathlon, said he was 'absolutely convinced this was a case of blatant cheating'. Onishenko was said to be 'dumbfounded' to discover that his foil was rigged. The Soviet team were disqualified, though Lednev and Mosolov were allowed to continue in individual competitions. The team gold medal was eventually awarded to Britain (and minutes after the ceremony Sergeant Fox was gathering signatures for a petition of clemency for his Russian opponent).

An observer noted at the time that the Soviet team's handbook – presumably owing to the quality of glue used in binding it – was the only fishy-smelling one among the dozens littering the press room.

AN ILL WIND

In the fourth innings of a baseball match at the Seattle Mariners' Kingdome in May 1981, while Seattle were playing the Kansas City Royals, Amos Otis bunted a ball down the third base line which came to rest right by the foul line. Instead of fielding the ball Lenny Randle, who was playing third base for Seattle, got down on his hands and knees, puffed out his cheeks and blew on the ball until it rolled over the line. Randle, who works as a comedian during the winter, got a great audience response.

The only person not amused was Kansas City Manager Jim Frey: the umpire ruled the ball foul and gave a strike to Otis. It took a great deal of discussion before Frey convinced the umpire to reverse the call and rule that Randle had interfered with the ball.

Seattle – or at least Randle – also received a lesson in the dangers of trying too hard: they lost to the Royals 8–3.

A GRATE FISHERMAN

The urge to fish may come upon a keen angler at the most awkward times: in the middle of the night, for instance, or while stuck in rush-hour traffic, or walking down the street. Constantly the fisherman is forced to sublimate his desires by thinking about what he caught the week before or, more probably, what he will catch next week if he gets a chance to fish on that special private stretch of river.

One autumn day in 1971 David Francis Long Pentecost of Rochdale, Lancashire set out to change all this. A policeman found him sitting on the pavement of a Rochdale street with the line of his fishing rod hanging down into the grating of a town drain. 'I am fighting for the right of anyone to fish where they like,' said Mr Pentecost. He was fined £5 for obstruction.

TALISMAN OVERBOARD

A yachtsman of world class, such as the protagonist of this story, will take enormous pains to see that his yacht is in first-class condition. The anchor, for example: although hardly likely to be used during a race (except in the event of a really major fiasco), it lets down the general tone of the craft if it is a rusty old horror – no matter how much money you may have spent on new suits of sails and internally-geared winches. It is of course a requirement that all yachts entered in Olympic events should carry an anchor, so why not spend a little extra and have a nice shiny new one?

Some such thought must have been in the mind of our hero when he entered the Spanish National Snipe Championships in

Malaga. He stayed right in the lead throughout the event, winning race after race. Everyone noticed his immaculate craft, and in particular his shiny new anchor, resplendent in its aluminium anti-fouling paint. Every night he would ceremoniously remove it from the yacht, place it in a little velvet bag, and take it back to his hotel. He would smile mysteriously, patting the bag and murmuring 'my lucky anchor'.

Some of his competitors became irritated at the way he would glide effortlessly past them, and his smug expression annoyed them. Sometimes he would even point at his 'lucky anchor' as he rounded a marker, leaving the others standing. One afternoon as he was tying up after a victorious race, one of the yachts he had defeated came up alongside.

'Lucky again, eh?' asked the helmsman in a none-too-friendly voice.

'Oh, well, you know. I have this talisman – it's never let me down so far.'

'Hasn't it just? Well, this time we're going to let *it* down!' and he leaped on board, seized the shiny object from the foredeck and hurled it as far as he could into the sea.

It floated. The 'lucky anchor', whose lightness had given him the edge in all those races, was made of balsawood – painted with aluminium anti-fouling paint.

2

Losing Your Cool

Never lose your cool: a fiasco is certain to follow. But it doesn't do to get too cool, or too excited either. Keep a level head at all times. One of the best ways of getting all mixed up is to consume a lot of alcohol while you are playing a game.

HEADS OR TAILS

The Russian oarsman Vyacheslav Ivanov was so delighted at winning the single sculls at Melbourne in 1956 that after the presentation ceremony he danced up and down, throwing his Olympic gold medal high into the air. Up, up it went, and *down*, straight into the waters of Lake Wendouree.

It is, one presumes, still there. Ivanov dived in after it, but never found it again, though he searched for hours. Professional divers were called in but they couldn't find it either.

Taking pity on the over-joyous sculler, the International Olympic Committee presented him with another, duplicate gold medal, and he went on to win a third at Rome in 1960. He hung on to that one.

CHAMPAGNE FOR A CHAMPION

The well-known Australian tennis player Randolph Lycett, who won the men's doubles at Wimbledon in 1921, 1922 and 1923, was seen refreshing himself liberally during the final set of a match against the Japanese Shimidzu at Wimbledon in 1920, which went to 10–8.

It was a hot day. Several times a liveried waiter appeared bearing a bucket of iced champagne. But what had Lycett been drinking beforehand to make him so thirsty? Some said it was brandy, others suspected gin. Whatever it was, its effects were long-lasting and powerful: after his defeat Lycett had to be carried off the court.

ALLETSON HITS OUT

The most ferocious burst of temperament ever displayed in county cricket was Alletson's dazzling performance in the Nottinghamshire vs. Sussex match at Hove in 1911.

This normally dull player suddenly completely lost his cool and became a demon batsman, hitting out at such a rate that fielders were injured and balls lost. The game finally had to be halted while efforts were made to prise the last available ball out of the soft woodwork of the pavilion. By this time sprained fingers and bruised shins abounded. Fatal injuries might well have been sustained had the Sussex eleven been rasher and bolder, but they were a prudent lot, and fairly soon got the measure of events. After the first few overs they adopted a policy of keeping out of the way of the ball as far as possible, and making sure it had come to rest before going near it.

Alletson's metamorphosis took place during lunch. Before lunch he had made 50 in an hour. Afterwards, last man in with Riley (ten not out) he proceeded, in the next fifteen minutes, to make another 50, and *89* in the fifteen minutes after that, for a total of 139 – a rate of 278 runs per hour: the highest ever achieved in county cricket.

Was it something he ate, or had he been stung into action by some personal slight? We shall never know. A large and hopeful crowd assembled to watch his subsequent performances at the Oval, but he never scored above 11 runs again, and was dropped from the Nottinghamshire side.

GETTING THERE

A problem which confronts every sportsman playing away from home is finding the field. For example, Mel Rose, a basketball referee from Oklahoma City, was to officiate at a game between Drake University and the US Air Force Academy at Colorado Springs a few years ago. Arriving at Denver Airport Mel made straight for the coffee stall. While he was drinking his coffee he got into conversation with a friendly soul who told him exactly how to find the Academy. Mel set off confidently for the bus station and took a bus to Colorado Springs. From there he rented a self-drive car and drove to the Academy, where he got a 'fine uncrowded view of the Academy's ultimate home now under construction'. After making inquiries he discovered that the game was actually being played in a temporary site back in Denver. He roared back down the freeway – only to be stopped by a highway patrolman for speeding and fined $104. He then realized he was never going to get to the game, so he turned round and took the next plane home.

Similarly unlucky were the four European skiers who flew to the States to take part in the Eastern Hotdog Championships in Waterville Valley, New Hampshire: Fuzzy and Ernst Garhaimen from Munich, Henri Authier from Paris and Paterlini Meschino from Switzerland. When they landed at Boston's Logan International Airport in the winter of 1974 they hired a taxi. 'Waterville' they pronounced cheerily, taking care to get the 'W' and the 'V' out clearly and in the right order. And to Waterville they went. Unfortunately, it was the Waterville in Maine, where there are no mountains – and no Hotdog Championships.

The little difficulty was soon sorted out, however, and off they drove again towards the setting sun – and New Hampshire. Their taxi bill was $200.

Perhaps the worst such mistake was made by five oarsmen

from Havana's Olimpicuba Club in 1964, due to compete in the International Rowing Regatta in Lucerne that July. Eventually Regatta officials received an abashed cable from Belgrade – 650 miles away. The oarsmen had thought Lucerne was in Yugoslavia.

THE ADMIRATION OF ROYALTY

Otway Woodhouse was knocking up at Wimbledon in 1880 when the Prince of Wales (the future Edward VII) happened to appear. The Prince watched Woodhouse for some time and, growing enthusiastic at the tennis player's ease and grace on the court, sent him his compliments.

During the game itself, against Herbert Lawford, Woodhouse was so intent on showing off his fancy, elegant strokes that he lost his concentration completely and was easily beaten.

Hearing that she was to play before Queen Mary during the 1926 Wimbledon Championships, the famous French champion Suzanne Lenglen became hysterical and refused to appear – or so the story went at the time. But the press of the day was unfair to Lenglen. What really happened was that the referee, F. R. Burrow, decided on the day before the match that in addition to the doubles scheduled for her that afternoon Lenglen should also play a singles against Mrs C. J. Dewhurst, so that Queen Mary could see her. Buckingham Palace was informed and Queen Mary replied that she would have an early luncheon and come down to watch the match. What Burrow failed to do, incredibly, was to inform Suzanne Lenglen.

Lenglen arrived at Wimbledon at 3.30, was asked to go on court at once and told that Queen Mary had been kept waiting an hour and a half. In the circumstances it is not surprising that the champion, due to play her doubles match at 4.30, became extremely upset and was in no condition to play tennis. The doubles match also had to be postponed, until the next day, when she and her partner Mlle Vlasto were beaten.

The public turned against their former idol, who was accused of throwing tantrums and of being rude to the Queen. On the following Monday, after reading the vituperations against her in the weekend press, she scratched from all events, and made no further appearances at Wimbledon that year.

FLOWERS FOR FERDINAND

Tempers in sport sometimes get out of hand and sportsmen loose their cool, but there are sports where *some* degree of ferocity is essential and a fiasco is likely to occur if blood temperatures never rise above zero in the first place. Take bullfighting.

Munro Leaf tells the story of Ferdinand the bull, who was too gentle to fight and preferred sniffing flowers. It is a pity that Ferdinand never encountered the matador Diego Bardon.

In his time Bardon had killed 100 bulls, but growing more intellectual and poetic he joined a movement with the curious name of 'Panic', which espoused peace, universal brotherhood and the development of new forms of artistic expression. Despite his membership in the group, however, and his growing reputation as an artist and writer, Bardon managed to get himself included on the bullfighting programme at the Vista Alegre ring in Madrid in April 1973.

As soon as he entered the ring it was obvious that Bardon's intentions were 'different'. First he threw a bunch of flowers at the bull. Then he bowed low to the spectators and began a sort of solo dance which in no way involved the animal. A titter went round the audience. Pausing to nibble at the flowers, the bull trotted off to the far side of the ring wearing a puzzled expression. Meanwhile the laughter of the crowd was giving way to boos and taunts, and finally the *aficionados* went berserk. It is an offence in Spanish law to refuse to kill a bull in a fight and Bardon was rescued from their fury only to be arrested and taken to prison.

The English, who count more admirers of Ferdinand among

their number than any other nation, came to Bardon's rescue. Alfred Weirs of Dartford, Kent, Secretary of the International Council Against Bullfighting, flew to Madrid on their behalf and paid the £175 fine. The bullfighter was released. A joyful scene took place in which Bardon declared that he had renounced for ever this cruel sport and would never kill another bull. Then, presenting Mr Weirs with a wooden sword, he made this touching observation: 'You see, fighting bulls are never mated. How doubly cruel it is that these bulls should die without ever knowing what it is to make love!'

'WRONG-WAY' RIEGLES

Ninety thousand partisan fans were packed into the Los Angeles Coliseum for the annual Rose Bowl Game on New Year's Day 1929 when the University of California was playing Georgia Tech for the national collegiate football championship. The game was hard-fought, neither team being able to take a commanding lead.

Late in the game, with California ahead by 7 to 6, Georgia Tech fumbled the ball deep in its own territory. In the wild scramble a California lineman, Roy Riegles, picked up the loose ball. Confused by the general mêlée, Riegles charged off like a rhinoceros.

Ninety thousand fans all started yelling at once: 'You're going the wrong way!' Riegles assumed they were cheering him on to a touchdown and redoubled his speed. California's backs raced down the field after him, hoping to overtake their teammate before he reached his destination. But by this time Riegles had the bit properly between his teeth and nothing was going to stop him. The roar of the crowd was in his ears and the thud of victory was in his heart. With a final surge he shook off a tackler and dived into the endzone – to score a safety.

The crowd could not believe what they had just seen: one of the greatest blunders in the history of sport. Riegles' score for the opposing side – two points – was enough to give Georgia Tech the championship.

Riegles' 'wrong-way' tag was later conferred upon an Irish pilot who made the greatest navigational error in the history of flying, Douglas Gorse Corrigan. Setting off at 10.15 from the Floyd Bennet field in New York on 17th July 1938, with compass carefully pre-set and course planned for California, Corrigan rose above the clouds and flew steadily on for 25 hours. Descending below cloud level he saw some low mountains and, assuming he had arrived, swept round for a closer look. But something in the configuration of the landscape told him this was not California. 'It was then that I realized I was over he remarked. 'The old compass had let me down.' He arrived in triumphant style at Baldonnel Aerodrome near Dublin after a flight totalling over 28 hours.

LILLEE SHILLY-SHALLIES

During the England vs. Australia Test of December 1979 at Perth the Australian fast bowler Dennis Lillee first introduced the aluminium bat he was promoting as a replacement for the familiar willow article. Greg Chappell, the team captain, was against it, on the grounds that it was actually not such a good bat. There was another difficulty: both men knew that new rules, specially redrafted to exclude aluminium bats, were at that moment at the printers. However, they had not yet come into force.

Lillee was determined to demonstrate his aluminium bat at all costs. When after a morning's play with the thing it was found that balls were being damaged, the English captain Mike Brearley objected. The umpire asked Lillee to change bats, but he refused. A noisy argument ensued in which everyone, including the spectators, told him in words of few syllables to grow up and get on with it. Far from giving way, Lillee walked off in high dudgeon. A few minutes later he reappeared, waving the same bat. Angry words were again exchanged; finally Chappell intervened and persuaded him to use a wooden one. Realizing that he had been worsted, Lillee tossed the offending aluminium object away.

Two days later, on 18th December, Lillee was caught for 19 runs. The names of the batsman, fielder and bowler then appeared on the scoreboard and formed a sort of childish jingle: 'Lillee caught Willey bowled Dilley'.

V FOR VICTORY

On at least two important sporting occasions the well-known 'victory' sign has been confused with the ruder two-fingered gesture. This happened to Tony Jarvis, the ex-captain of the British Olympic swimming team, at the Amateur Swimming Association Championships in August 1970. Jarvis had already been given an undertaking not to indulge in political gestures following a protest he made against the supply of arms to South Africa when Prime Minister Edward Heath was visiting the Commonwealth Games in Edinburgh earlier that year. But he was finally dropped from the team after a gesture of another kind made at the end of the ASA Championships.

In the men's 100 yards freestyle finals Jarvis swam less well than usual and came only third. The crowd booed and he made a two-fingered gesture at them before stalking off. He later remarked: 'I certainly did not make a rude sign with my fingers at the crowd as I walked away. My hand was raised with two fingers, pointing, with the back of my hand towards me. Surely this is recognized now as the sign for peace.'

Eventually a somewhat shamefaced Jarvis returned to the poolside to stand beside the winner, Malcolm Windeatt, and shake his hand as the medals were presented. But he remained recalcitrant, and refused to allow his photograph to be taken, or to repeat his 'sign for peace'.

Just over a year later at Hickstead, Sussex an even more notable 'V' sign fiasco occurred. The perpetrator was Harvey Smith, the well-known showjumper, who had just won the W. D. & H. O. Wills Show Jumping Derby. On completing the winning round of the jump-off, Smith turned to the directors' box and made a gesture. The crowd guffawed, and it was this perhaps as much as the act itself which angered the judges. It should be said that they were predisposed to feel irritated towards Smith: he had left the Jumping Derby Cup behind at his home in Bingley, Yorkshire – he had won it the year before – and there was some anxiety about whether it would turn up, on a train, in time for the presentation ceremony. It did; and was given straight back to Smith by Douglas Bunn, with the words 'Well done'. But later that day the £2,000 prize money was declared forfeit and the judges sent Smith a telegram saying he had been disqualified.

There was much speculation about what had really happened, and about exactly what message the telegram contained. Bernard Levin in *The Times* suggested various possible texts, from 'YOUR CONDUCT UNBECOMING OFFICER, GENTLEMAN AND SHOWJUMPER' to 'WHY YOU FILTHY BRUTE JUST YOU WAIT'. It actually said 'BECAUSE OF YOUR DISGUSTING GESTURE THE DIRECTORS AND I HAVE DISQUALIFIED YOU', and was signed by Douglas Bunn, who had presented the Cup. He had not seen the gesture in question himself, and only agreed to the disqualification after seeing a television replay.

Harvey Smith was not in the least contrite: his gesture was the Churchillian 'V' sign, made in a friendly and victorious spirit. 'They tell me I never smile when I win,' he said, 'and now they take me the wrong way.' He went on to make the somewhat unfortunate analogy that if a footballer scores a goal and then punches the referee, the goal is not disallowed.

Two days later the judges relented and set aside their decision. They had acted wrongly, they announced, in not first giving Smith an opportunity to appear before them and explain his action. There was a further fiasco when the film of the gesture was lost and then refound, but eventually everything was smoothed out and peace – with honour – was restored to the showjumping world.

LAMBS DRESSED AS WOLVES

In 1973 the Oxbarn Social Club amateur football team, of the Wolverhampton Sunday League, saved up for a tour of the Continent, intending to play the odd local match here and there along the way. They had booked two matches in Germany and upon arriving at Mainz on 15th August were surprised to find that the local team had invited them to play in a stadium. It looked a pretty expensive stadium at that. 'They spare no expense, these Germans,' they thought. This feeling was confirmed when they learned that the opposing players were on an £80 bonus to win. And outside the stadium there were queues of spectators waiting to get in.

Play began, not without some trepidation among the Oxbarn team. Before long the German side had scored their first goal. And their second. And their third... It was a massacre. Whenever Oxbarn succeeded in getting the ball into enemy territory – which was not very often – a great cheer would go up from the crowd. In no time at all the ball would be back at their end, heading for the goal again.

The Oxbarn Social Club lost, sadly, 21 goals to nil: after the 20th goal the Oxbarn goalkeeper stayed on his knees, praying for the final whistle.

'At least the German crowd cheered us when we managed to cross the halfway line,' said Ron Parker, the Club secretary. Everything had suddenly become hideously clear to him when he saw the billings outside the ticket office: SVW MAINZ vs. WOLVERHAMPTON WANDERERS.

A REVIVING NIP

One of this century's greatest champions and supporters of swimming was Lord Freyberg, who until his death in 1963 was President of the Channel Swimming Association. He was fond of telling the following story about his own Channel swim fiasco, which took place shortly after the end of the First World War.

The crossing started well, although the sea was rougher than he had anticipated, and the action of the waves became increasingly exhausting. As the coast of France came slowly into sight he became more and more tired and finally, a mere 300 yards from the shore, was unable to swim any further. His wife, who had been following in a support boat, uncorked a flask of brandy and persuaded him to swallow some. This had a restorative effect, but also resulted in the complete loss of his navigational faculties. The boat followed his floundering efforts round and round, in ever decreasing circles, until at last he was persuaded to desist and dragged from the water, 'as weak as a kitten and as drunk as a Lord'.

BEER TENT BLAMED

It is not necessary for a sportsman to actually drink himself in order to experience the devastating effects of alcohol on co-ordination, timing and muscular strength.

In the tense final match of the England vs. Rest of the World golf tournament at Pannal near Harrogate in August 1972, Jack Newton of Australia was neck-and-neck against Tony Jacklin. Jacklin was one-up at the eighteenth hole but pitched his ball over the green: it took him three more strokes to hole out. Just as he was poised over the ball the beer tent, barely 30 yards away, shook with gales of laughter. Some wag had cracked a joke, and the alcoholic hilarity that ensued, vibrating through the intervening space, completely destroyed Jacklin's concentration.

'I should have stopped,' he said later. 'I tried to cut the ball right up in the air but I hit it thin.'

The 22-year-old Newton won the hole in par 4 and the game ended in a tie. Thus was Jacklin deprived of victory in the £15,000 Double Diamond Golf Tournament by another man's beer and another fool's laughter.

FAST, STRONG AND VERY VERY LONG

At the first World Swimming Championships at Belgrade in 1973 there was a great fuss over the exact length of the pool: the Belgrade Geophysical Institute was called in for a special measuring session using the latest sonar techniques, and indeed the pool was found to be slightly too long. To compensate the electronic touch-timing board was moved in by one centimetre.

Steve Holland, the 15-year-old Australian competing in the 1500 metres freestyle event, started out at such a pace that by the time he had completed the first 16 lengths of the 50-metre pool he had broken the 800 metre world record by 6.2 seconds – with another 14 lengths still to go. Everyone round the pool became so absorbed in watching this seemingly inexhaustible human dolphin swimming length after length that when the time came to blow the warning whistle on his penultimate lap this important detail was forgotten. Holland reached the 1500 metres point and a cheer went up: *another* world record by 14.8 seconds – a total time of just 15 minutes 31.85 seconds! But Holland, head spinning with the frenzy of the race, took no notice of the cheer, nor of the frantic signals to stop. On he swam, back to the other end. Here people tried again to stop him, but again he turned, did yet another length, and turned again . . . Then, at last, something must have registered amid the confusion, for a few strokes down on the third extra length he stopped and left the pool.

For minutes afterwards Holland reeled round in a daze. As well he might: after all the fuss over one silly centimetre he had swum 120 metres too far, and still broken two world records.

THE WRONG CARD

On the final day of the US Masters Championship at Augusta in 1968, the Argentine Champion Roberto de Vicenzo played with a brilliance rarely equalled in professional golf. It was his forty-fifth birthday. On his final round on one of the toughest courses in the world he scored an eagle with a nine iron at the first hole, followed by birdies at the second, third, twelfth, fifteenth and seventeenth.

It was on the fatal seventeenth hole that it happened. American television was broadcasting to an audience of around ten million viewers, and all of them could see the final putt of three. De Vicenzo was now tied for first place with Bob Goalby: Tommy Aaron, who was scoring, gave him the card to sign – which is just what he did. But Aaron had put down a four instead of a three, and de Vicenzo's failure to notice this incorrect detail lost him the Championship on a technicality.

He refused to question the decision and stoically put it down to his own carelessness. In his words: 'I think, you are professional, you no want to make this kind of mistake. When you make mistake on the golf course, you have chance to recover, but when you make mistake on the scorecard, you cannot say anything, you cannot blame anyone; you have to take the responsibility and inside you feel very bad. I felt very bad for months.'

De Vicenzo, whose charm and good humour have made him immensely popular among all who follow golf, was later presented both with the Bobby Jones Award and with the William D. Richardson award for sportsmanship by the American golf writers. A presentation dinner was held, to which de Vicenzo came specially from the Argentine. On his arrival at Miami a customs officer asked him if he were going to New York for business. 'No,' he replied, 'for dinner.'

At the dinner he discovered that his name had been

misspelled in a variety of peculiar ways: on the seating list, on the menu, on the trophy itself (Di Vicenzo, de Vincenzo, di Vincenzo . . .). Bob Hope, who was master of ceremonies, asked de Vicenzo to make a speech and this is what he said:

'I be honoured for signing wrong scorecard. Now my name is spelled wrong three times by writers. That's all I have to say.'

It brought the house down.

VODKA ON THE ROCKS

Scandinavia is the best motor rally territory on earth. In the summer there are the long winding forest roads, mostly unmade and full of stones and dust. In the winter rivers, lakes and even the sea freeze over, and the drivers stage their rallies on the frozen surface. Studded tyres are used to grip the ice, and the top layer of snow has to be swept away by a snowplough.

The route of the 1981 Karlstadt Rally in Värmland Province, Sweden, was along a wide frozen river. To clear the track an Autocross champion was given a grader to drive, making his own bends as the fancy took him. He was also given a bottle of

vodka, both to keep him warm and to encourage him to make some sharp and fancy curves in the track.

Halfway along the route there was a power station, which took its cooling water from the river. No one quite knew how safe the ice was around the station, but emboldened by the vodka the Autocross champion took his grader too close, and down he went. When they came to get him they found him sitting on top of his cab, which barely projected from the surrounding ice, with a happy smile on his face and an empty bottle of vodka firmly clutched in one hand.

BAD TIMING

Surinam sent only one representative to the Rome Olympics in 1960: a runner named Wim Essajas who was entered for the 800 metres event. Having travelled all the way from South America to Rome he was in a somewhat exhausted state, and decided to put in as much rest as he could before the race. He snoozed serenely through the morning at the Olympic Village, woke full of energy and confidence, ate a light lunch and arrived at the stadium prepared to show the world what Surinam could do. He was greeted with the news that the 800 metres event was over – it had been run that morning. The runner's fury at this irretrievable error can well be imagined, and focused upon Freddy Glans, Surinam's 'team leader', who after all had only one athlete to worry about. A disconsolate Essajas set off on the long trip back to South America – not forgetting to file a lawsuit against the spearhead of Surinam's Olympic hopes.

Twelve years later three American sprinters were sitting in a room in the Munich Olympic village after lunch watching television, resting before their event, the second round of the 100 metres, which, as they had firmly fixed in their minds, was scheduled for 5.00. At a quarter to three the sprinters received the shock of their lives when they heard their race being announced on television: they had confused 15.00 with 5.00! An unscheduled pre-race sprint then took place to get to the stadium in time for the start. Only one of them made it: R. Taylor – and he won the silver medal. Judging from his dash to the stadium he deserved the gold.

COX'S FOLLY

Queen's College, Oxford boasts a high proportion of hefty north-countrymen among its undergraduates, which does much to explain why the college has always enjoyed such success on the river. This tradition goes back to 1837, when Queen's, head of the river, took on and defeated St John's College, Cambridge in a 'prototype' of Henley Regatta. Few spectators were there to witness that historic race.

Rather more spectators indeed were present – though uninvited – when the writer Count Adam Zamoyski coxed a Queen's College eight in 1967. A first-year undergraduate, Zamoyski had already taken the eight out on half a dozen occasions, but this time the coach suggested they should go for a longer row, above Folly Bridge and along the river in the direction of Port Meadow.

The river goes into some sharp meanders as it approaches Folly Bridge. Simultaneously the current accelerates, making this a difficult area for an inexperienced cox. As the eight approached the first bend Zamoyski began to get anxious: the boat did not appear to respond properly to the rudder. (What was happening was that the crew, also inexperienced, were beginning to tire, and failed to keep the boat moving fast enough to overtake the current, so that the boat started to lose way.) At the second bend things got worse. 'Row!' screamed Zamoyski, but to no avail: they had lost steerage way and the eight was beginning to slew at an alarming angle. By the time they reached the bridge they were broadside on, and crashed sideways into it, to hoots of laughter from the large crowd who had gathered to watch the fun.

Zamoyski's last memory of his final appearance as cox before he abandoned sport for literature was of a beefy Lancashire undergraduate clinging to the end of an oar, which was slowly being raised into the air by the leverage of the boat as it pressed into the masonry of the bridge, shouting at the top of his voice: 'Help! I can't swim!'

3

Spectators, Supporters and Fans

Serious sportsmen have always found spectators a nuisance, but increasingly the roles of both are being reversed. The public meets famous sportsmen in all sorts of places and situations outside the stadium as well as inside. Fiascos result. And spectators are beginning to cast off convention and come out in the open, baring their breasts to the world.

FIRED WITH ENTHUSIASM

During a football match in Syracuse, Sicily on 4th January 1974 the referee made the classic error of sending off a local player for a foul. This is something you just don't do in Sicily if you value your health.

A fan who took his loyalty to his team really to heart left at this juncture, returning ten minutes later with a double-barrelled hunting gun. After firing several shots into the air he pointed the gun at the referee and demanded the reinstatement of the player. The linesmen ran for their lives. The referee, whose awareness of his predicament was by this time extremely keen, agreed. Well, when a Sicilian soccer fan points a gun at you, you do agree.

The visiting side from Northern Italy were not used to this sort of thing, and their goalkeeper didn't like the way the fan, uttering strange Sicilian oaths, kept pointing the gun at him – between swigs from his wine flask. He was so shaken that he let in seven goals.

After the match the wielder of the gun could not be found. He had been carried away by some cronies on a donkey cart, dead drunk.

CHURCHILL MANIA

In February 1946 a spectator at a baseball game managed not only to distract the attention of a crowd of 30,000 but to bring the entire proceedings to a halt. What is more, the crowd enjoyed every minute of it.

During the early months of this first post-war year Winston

and Clementine Churchill were taking a well-earned rest, relaxing in the sun at Miami and touring through Cuba and the United States. (Churchill made a number of official visits and speeches, including the famous one at Fulton, Missouri in which he immortalized the phrase 'iron curtain'.)

The couple spent much of February in Cuba, staying with some friends who had a private beach. Everyone on the island was anxious to welcome the great man, and various reports of his appearance at functions were circulating among the population, though he in fact kept very quiet apart from the official reception itself. Thus it was with tremendous enthusiasm that the news was received during a baseball game attended by a large crowd in Havana that Mr Churchill was among the spectators. A portly figure smoking a cigar was spotted in a box high in the stands, and as the rumour spread and people started to turn round the figure was seen to make the familiar 'V' sign. An announcement went out over the loudspeaker: 'Ladies and gentlemen, we have among us this afternoon Mr Winston Churchill.'

Play stopped at once. A wave of delirious cheering and clapping swept through the crowd, and police guarding the field rushed to the stands. Reporters and photographers, instantly alerted, hurried from their offices to the stadium. Meanwhile, to the delight of the crowd, the man in the box started shaking hands with all those nearest to him. Then out came the autograph books. Suddenly a roar of another kind went up. The signatures were not Churchill's at all: the man in the stand was a practical joker who, taking advantage of a certain physical resemblance, and dressing in suitable clothes, had decided to play a hoax on Havana. The crowd burst out laughing, whistles and cheers filled the air, the reporters went home, and the game was resumed.

THE ANKLE SLAM

Although no complaint was ever raised, Cyril Tolley lost to Bobby Jones in the Amateur Golf Championship at St Andrews in 1930 only because of the freak intervention of a spectator's ankle.

Jones's second shot to the road hole, intentionally hit to the left of the bunker, was a little too hard. It struck the foot of a spectator, bounded off onto the green, and Jones was able to hole it in a couple of putts. Jones was lucky: if the spectator hadn't been where he was the ball would certainly have gone well into the rough. The man concerned was less lucky: he suffered a bruised ankle. And Cyril Tolley was very unlucky indeed: the two players were all square throughout the match and Jones only won at the 19th because of a stymie.

A CLERICAL BELT

It was 1 a.m. on a chilly January night in 1965. The Dean of Bocking was in his study, working on a sermon. He heard a scuffling sound. No matter – what was that verse in Ecclesiastes?

Oh vestibules, there it goes again . . . better go and investigate.

Advancing into the garden with a torch he soon made out the form of a young intruder cowering against the wall. He remonstrated. The young man expostulated. Violence ensued. (The Dean of Bocking is not a big man.) There was a muffled cry and a tinkle of glass as a body smashed into the cold frame.

Describing the incident the following day, the 5 foot 3 inch Dean, the Very Reverend Kenneth Wade (50 at the time), remarked: 'I have told the young man I shall take no further action. He attacked me and I threw him over my shoulder. I am sorry he has hurt his arm.'

The Very Reverend Kenneth Wade is an expert at judo.

MOBHANDED

Henry Cooper was on his way back to Chislehurst from a meal at the well-known Thomas à Becket pub in the Old Kent Road on the eve of a major fight in 1968. His brother George, also a famous boxer, was driving, and with them was Henry's manager Jimmy Wicks. It was a dark, wet night, and as they made a left turn out of the main road an elderly gentleman on a bicycle swerved in front of them. George braked, and though they did not actually hit the cyclist he wobbled off his machine.

Picking himself up and cursing roundly, the man advanced towards the Coopers' car with clenched fists and a menacing expression. Henry got out, then George, and then Jimmy, who is not exactly a seven stone weakling himself.

'All right,' said the angry cyclist, eyeing them and dropping his fists. 'Just because you're mobhanded.'

And he turned round, walked back to his bicycle and pedalled away, never realizing who it was that he had offered to fight.

A SOLEMN MOMENT

In the majority of sporting events the spectator makes a voluntary effort to appear, often paying large sums for the privilege. There are some sports, however, such as water-skiing, which are witnessed by people who have no interest whatever in the goings-on, and often regard it as something of an intrusion on the natural scenery.

When one is sitting at anchor in a yacht in some lonely and clear-watered bay, listening to the gentle lapping of the waves, with a glass of Muscadet in one hand and a chicken leg in the other, there can be nothing more infuriating than the sudden intrusion of a screaming power boat trailing some inanely grinning idiot on skis. The noise shatters the nerves and the wash from the boat spills the Muscadet and sends the chicken leg flying into the bilges. It is no use shaking a clenched fist and calling them rude names: the waterskier will think you are waving encouragement and probably get the boat to come even closer next time so that he can show off his technique going backwards or with one leg in the air.

Balloons, however, unless motorized, are comparatively harmless even to the unintentional observer. In fact their brightly-coloured shapes suspended in the sky on a clear summer evening add a rather picturesque quality to the landscape of Wiltshire or the South Downs. The balloonist Anthony Smith tells the story of one such summer evening when with four companions he sailed blithely over the English countryside, shouting for joy at all who passed on the earth below.

As they floated on, a village appeared dead ahead with a church, a line of chestnuts, and thatched roofs. They decided to descend for a closer look. There seemed to be a great many people about – some sort of procession or fête, perhaps. They would go right down to the centre of the fête, they thought, and shout out in a Bacchanalian manner, and then, waving at the earthbound merrymakers they would drop some sand ballast on their silly heads as they soared off up again into the sky. This was the plan.

They slowly approached, the wind dropping all the time, calling out all sorts of hilarious, rude and festive messages. But no one looked up, and no one answered. They recited limericks and made farmyard noises. Still there was no response. As they crept very slowly past a line of trees they suddenly realized the reason. It was a funeral. There were the mourners, the flower-decked coffin, and the freshly-dug grave.

The balloon's progress slowed still further and they hung, monstrous, bright orange and motionless, above the lych gate. It was a solemn moment. The wind had dropped and even the jackdaws had retreated into the trees. The silence was fearful, and all the balloonists could do was to pretend desperately not to be there. But they *were* there, moving in funereal step with the procession, and getting lower every second. If they were not very careful they were going to hit the church tower. The only remedy was sand (it was a hydrogen balloon), and at this late stage in the descent it would have to be dumped overboard by the sackful. They simply could not bring themselves to drop it onto the mourners, or, worse still, into the gaping hole of the grave which they were now directly above. But if they collided with the church tower, the balloon would be almost sure to burst, catch fire and probably take the church with it in the conflagration. In Anthony Smith's words:

> 'The tower loomed. The mourners mourned. The disaster approached most effortlessly. There was nothing now to be done, save to pour two sackfuls of sand onto the slated roof beneath us. The noise was unforgettable. The jackdaws leapt into the air. The procession had to look up. Dislodged slates rattled slowly down that steep-sided roof, and kept up their own clatter for an age before falling to the ground, one by one.
> '"Sorry," I said, "terribly sorry."'

In abashed silence, they floated away.

GRAB AND SMASH

In Detroit, just before Christmas 1968, a well-built man emerged from a bank carrying a valuable-looking bag. His air was nonchalant, and he carried the bag lightly, as though it contained no more than a couple of sponges and a pair of satin trunks.

An ugly-looking character lurking round the corner was of a different opinion concerning the contents: anyone carrying bags out of banks is carrying money. Pulling out a knife he told the man to hand it over. Alex Venettis, a former Golden Gloves heavyweight champion, did just that. Staggering under the weight of $400 in coins, his attacker fell backwards, clutching the spoil with both hands. And Venettis knocked him out with a right.

STREAKERS

A commentator who prefers to remain anonymous has given me the following invaluable insight into streaking: 'Streaking is an aberration dreamed up by a lot of hippies in one of the less disciplined American universities during the early Seventies. The root causes are of interest. Sport today is increasingly divided into two camps: the tiny handful of stars who perform, and the vast *lumpenproletariat* who spectate. In the same way that in this sexually perverse age those who watch intimate acts on the screen far outnumber those who perform them, so in sport we have become a world of *voyeurs*. The deep tensions which this creates reach from time to time an exhibitionistic *node* which, gathering psychological momentum from the collective unconscious repressions of the spectating mass, erupts unstoppably into a hyperkinetic act of symbolic personal nudity.'

I could not have put it better myself.

The history of streaking is divided, of course, into two quite distinct eras: the early 'generalized' streak and the later, strictly sport-orientated displays. (I have been told of a third category of streaker, always female, who manifests herself by the side of rally and motor racing tracks, but I put this down largely to the overheated imagination of exhausted drivers.)

Pioneer streaks were conducted by a handful of students in California and Florida during the autumn of 1973 and by January 1974 the first European streaker had been reported: a young Belgian cycled along a road near Ghent, completely naked, to fetch some chips. He won a 400 Franc bet, but was arrested, fined 3,000 Francs and jailed for a month. This harsh punishment temporarily cooled European interest but great progress was being made in the United States: by the middle of

February 1974 multiple outbreaks were taking place. At Boulder, Colorado 1,200 naked students ran round a quadrangle, watched by 5,000 fellow scholars and local residents. The 1,000-student streak at Athens, Georgia was witnessed by over 20,000 people. (Some of these mass streaks became confused with rioting and there were many arrests.)

In March 1974 a lone representative of the financial world, a 28-year-old bond broker, ran through Wall Street in only his shoes and socks but, alas, streaking has so far proved to have little relevance in a monetary context.

As for sport, some early incidents had paved the way. In the Fifties a boxer appeared at a South London Amateur Club Exhibition fight, removed his dressing-gown, and revealed to all present that he had neglected to put on his shorts. There were also some odd goings-on at the Lakeside Golf Club, Los Angeles in the summer of 1958. The club newsletter, published in the spring of the following year, states: 'Because of the greatly increased play on the golf course by both sexes the board of directors has voted to require all men golfers to wear covering above the belt line.'

Then, in the winter of 1973–74, four members of the Illinois Sport Parachute Club bailed out over the University of Illinois in nothing but their parachutes, helmets and shoes. Meanwhile in England there were signs of an imminent outbreak in the very heart of one of the nation's most hallowed institutions: a *Times* leader writer had been seen not wearing a waistcoat.

Events followed swiftly and Europe began to feel the full force of the contagion: Paris (Eiffel Tower) 8th March; Wiesbaden 8th March, then England. On 9th March 1974 at Bedford Town Football Club the first recorded sports streaker was greeted with applause by 3,000 spectators before being hustled into a car by police. Meanwhile a man in Essex had done 400 yards in Braintree High Street in only his shoes and socks for a £40 bet.

Further outbreaks of non-sport streaking were reported throughout the weekend, and news flashes poured in from Milan, Heidelberg, even Taipei. In Belfast five men and two women streaked through churchgoers in Donegal Square; there were further outbreaks in Hull and Derby, and then word came of the backlash in Florida, cradle of the streaking movement: a group of fully clothed people had streaked through a nudist camp.

March 17th saw the famous 'Kingston Bridge' streak, in which the 'Kingston Seven' caused a furore at Kingston-upon-Thames, Surrey as they prevented traffic from crossing the river for a full half-hour. A woman of 21 who described herself as a 'display artist' was arrested.

By this time the trend was clear. Streaking was becoming recognized as part of sport. A hardy pioneer, to prove this point, appeared on the nursery slopes of a skiing resort at Carrbridge in the Cairngorms, wearing nothing but ski boots and a pair of skis. And on 23rd April a bearded, 26-year-old Australian, Michael O'Brien, who was living in Fulham, streaked across the field at Twickenham during the half-time interval of the England vs. France Rugby International. A policeman was after him – in a flash – and demonstrated a hitherto unknown use for the constabulary helmet as an instrument of concealment. For this historic act O'Brien was, unbelievably, not awarded a medal as 'First Twickenham Streaker' but fined £10 for insulting behaviour. England lost the match with one penalty goal and a try to France's three goals and two tries – and, one is tempted to add, deservedly.

After this, streaking became a regular item on the calendar of sporting fiascos. One who did much to establish its credentials (and his own) was the first streaker to appear at Lord's Cricket Ground. It was the fourth of August 1975. The weather was extremely hot, and there were signs that something might be about to happen when, to the distress of the Secretariat, in the Long Room of the Pavilion even some of the most traditional members began to remove their jackets and ties. Then, magnificently symbolizing the collective unconscious wishes of all those present, a man appeared wearing nothing but plimsolls and socks, streaked towards the grandstand, turned right, ran down the pitch towards the Nursery End, and did the splits over both sets of stumps. The deed was done during the interval of play, and was greeted with applause and laughter. Greg Chappell whacked the streaker on the behind as he passed. Alan Knott, who was batting, was standing at the stumps at the time, and later remarked to cricket commentator Brian Johnston that it was the first time he had ever seen two balls coming down the pitch at him!

Another hurdling streaker was seen at Perth on 19th December 1975, during the West Indian Test. This streaker was totally nude, and did not even wear anything on his feet. Admiring, lightly-clad female spectators looked on as he leaped over the stumps, risking all. In the background, advertisement hoardings proclaimed 'City's make it easy'. Although this streaker was warmly applauded by the crowd, he did nothing for the morale of the Australian team, who lost by an innings and 87 runs.

Of the many other streakers of recent years one who deserves a mention for originality was the man who appeared at Wembley on 8th May 1976 when St Helens were playing Widnes in the Rugby League Cup Final. It was the start of the very hot summer of 1976 – a vintage year for streakers. The 'Wembley Conductor', as streaking historians have dubbed this individual, managed to climb onto the crossbar of the goal, from which vantage point he conducted the band, thus becoming the first musical streaker. Police and photographers looked on until the performance was over, whereupon he climbed down unprotestingly. Pedants have questioned his place in the history of streaking, on the grounds that he preserved a degree of modesty by retaining not only his socks but also a pair of boxer shorts; nevertheless no serious account of the streaking phenomenon can ignore his contribution.

Later the same year in Montreal, at the closing ceremony of the 21st Olympiad, a streaker made a brief and elegant appearance, weaving in and out among the dancing gymnasts in such a way that it would have been impossible to stop him without spoiling the whole performance. This streaker, who was seen on television by millions all over the world, was totally nude – 'not even wearing his identity card' as Lord Killanin remarked at the time.

As I write, the latest and perhaps most highly appreciated of all streakers on the English sporting scene is Erica Roe, who made her appearance at Twickenham on Saturday 2nd January 1982. The occasion was a Rugby International between England and Australia, and during a half-time interval, just as England's captain Bill Beaumont was trying to get his side to concentrate on the pep-talk he was giving them, Erica tore off her blouse and dashed onto the pitch. The effect on the England side was instantaneous. The more Beaumont ranted and raved, the more the players laughed. Turning round to see what was so funny, he remarked: 'God, they are big, aren't they,' and went on with his talk. Meanwhile 68,000 spectators watched as Erica streaked across the pitch, with everything bouncing and bobbing and two policemen in hot pursuit. The policemen, grinning broadly, finally captured their prey and managed to conceal one of her assets with her blouse, and the other with the well-tried helmet technique. Although millions witnessed the scene on television critics have complained that 'coverage was not good'.

The following Monday Erica's place of work, the Westwood Bookshop in Petersfield, was besieged by sightseers and reporters hoping to catch another glimpse of this highly talented performer. Erica eventually left the world of books to take up some of the many new opportunities which beckoned after her sudden rise to fame – one of which was modelling men's double-breasted suits at £125 a day.

ROYAL FLUSH

Among the multitude of small boats bobbing about on the waters of the Solent hoping to see some of the sailing at Cowes in 1978 was a 22-foot fibreglass 'weekender' called *Seal*. This particular *Seal*, riding rather low in the water with eleven people on board, was the prototype of the class, designed by the late Angus Primrose, who was there that day with his wife, children, Polly Drysdale, Angela Kirby, and various young men in high spirits and pretty girls in bikinis. It was warm and sunny, so the party set off for lunch and a swim in Osborne Bay.

Before they had got very far out of Cowes glasses were filled and a general sense of *bonhomie* prevailed. So many sails of every size and shape were visible and so many craft were crossing each other's tracks that they were not surprised to be hailed by two young men in a Flying Fifteen who seemed to be in trouble. They had broken their rudder, one of the young men explained: could *Seal* possibly give them a tow back to their mooring? This was, of course, the last thing anyone wanted to do on such a nice day, with a party under way and the prospect of lunch and a swim close at hand. Primrose replied in tones of hearty rebuke:

'Sorry, old chap, but when I was your age I learned how to sail myself home without a rudder. If you don't learn now you never will. There's no way I'm going to turn back at this stage and waste everyone's morning towing back every Tom, Dick and Harry who gets into trouble.'

On they sailed.

Finally, amid much jollity, they reached their destination and dropped anchor, and by the time most of the party had had a dip and preparations were in hand for lunch it was well into the afternoon. Suddenly Primrose noticed a familiar boat anchored not far away: Admiral Morrice McMullen's 32-foot wooden yacht *Fidget* (built in 1910). In contrast to the fairly orgiastic scene now visible on *Seal* everything aboard *Fidget* looked quiet and sedate. A group of well-dressed people were on board drinking tea. Feeling that it was rather boring of them to be drinking tea so early in the afternoon – it was barely four o'clock – Primrose cried out cheerily: 'Ahoy there, Morrice, what are you doing with that dreary-looking crowd? Why not come over and join us and have some fun?'

The Admiral's reply was diplomatically non-committal – even a trifle chilling.

Eventually everyone decided to get a bit nearer the action: 'Let's go and have a look at *Britannia*,' someone said, and off they went. As the Royal Yacht's massive hull loomed closer there was a sudden change in wind direction. Primrose, his nose in a gin and tonic at this point, realized that action was called for. 'Lee-ho!' he shouted. Polly Drysdale, at the helm, slammed the tiller over hard – and collided with *Britannia* just aft of the companionway.

'We thought you might be the party coming aboard for tea,' joked a rating as he helped push them off with a boathook.

'No, I'm afraid we'll never get invited if we carry on like that,' replied Primrose.

There is some conflict of opinion about what happened after that. Was there a second collision – or perhaps a near-miss – with HMS *Leopard*, the destroyer on guard? Several present do remember being rather too close to a SAM missile for comfort, and everyone agrees that a concoction known as 'Shangri-la' (like Sangria but with brandy and curacao added) was produced. And drunk. Several observers at one point called out encouragingly to the lady at *Seal*'s helm: 'Carry on, Polly, we think you're doing *awfully* well!'

That evening at Dot's bar one of the first bits of news Primrose heard was that Prince Andrew had lost his rudder in the Flying Fifteen race and someone had refused him a tow. Then a voice said: 'Did you see Morrice McMullen had Princess Alexandra and her children on board *Fidget* for tea?' The following day, as everyone crowded into the Groves and Gutteridge tent in the pouring rain, news of the triple clangers quickly spread and was just as quickly dubbed 'Primrose's hat trick'.

'Well done, skipper,' remarked the cartoonist Andrew Spedding, clapping Primrose on the back. 'You won't get the OBE this year!'

CHANGING THE GUARD

At Henley in 1979 a number of supporters paid the penalty for over-enthusiasm.

The Irish Garda had sent an eight to compete in the Prince Philip Challenge Cup – presumably more in the belief that it would prove a pleasant weekend for the lads than out of any covetousness for cups. As it transpired, though, the stamina of the Garda Siochana Boat Club won the day, and the victorious oarsmen were greeted by a crowd of cheering Garda men thronging the rickety landing stage. Whether through the vigour of their welcoming gestures, or sheer constabulary weight, their assembled presence proved too much for the wooden stage: it collapsed, throwing at least twenty men into the Thames.

Luckily it was sunny, and for several hours afterwards the Garda were to be seen spreading out their clothes and belongings on the banks of the river – including, of course, their wallets. Folding currency of various denominations was carefully laid out to dry on the grass. The men then took turns to stand round the assortment of steaming underwear and pound notes – an Irish version of changing the guard known as 'guarding the change'.

4

Officials, Referees and Umpires

If there's no other obvious cause for a fiasco, it's probably the fault of the man who organized the event. If he's not to blame, you can usually get some fun out of venting your anger on the referee.

TECHNICAL ERRORS

The 1904 Olympic Games at St Louis, Missouri were probably the least efficiently organized ever held. As in Paris in 1900 the Games coincided with a World Fair, and in many people's minds the two functions became confused. Attendance was poor, and the spirit of Olympic competition was marred by tacking on a curious 'anthropological' sideshow, in which Patagonians, Filipinos, Ainus, Mexican Coropas and even pygmies performed a parody athletic meeting. A pygmy, summoning all his strength, managed to heave the shot exactly three metres.

The organizers could not perhaps be blamed for the marathon runner – a Cuban postman named Felix Carvagal – who turned up at the race in a nightshirt. Despite stopping en route to joke and chat with spectators and stealing some peaches from an orchard he still placed fourth. Nor were they responsible for the wild dog which chased two South African entrants two miles off the course. They could, however, have taken a little more trouble over the hurdles.

After winning the 400 metres hurdles in a record time of 53 seconds, the American Harry Hillman was told that he could not claim the record, because he had knocked down the last hurdle. Hillman retorted that it could never have been a record anyway: the organizers had made the hurdles only 76 centimetres (30 inches) high instead of the regulation 91.4 centimetres (36 inches).

Perhaps the worst official lapse occurred in the start of the 200 metres men's race. Three times the starter fired his gun, and three times someone broke ranks. The judge then addressed the four men angrily and told them that if they couldn't all make a decent, clean start he would punish them by giving them an extra metre to run. Thus the four finalists found themselves lined up a metre behind the starting line, and the winner, the American Archie Hahn, can claim to be the holder of a unique Olympic record: the 201 metres. He did it in 21.6 seconds.

UMPIRE TAKES UMBRAGE

The unpopularity of umpires and referees is amazing. They are quite indispensable to most games, they work selflessly for very little reward, are scarcely ever unfair or vindictive, and yet they are not loved.

Signor Troni of Piacenza is an example. He went down to Caserta to act as referee in a soccer match between Catanzaro and Caserta in September 1969. The Caserta team, the hosts, had been accused of bribery in a recent game and relegated to third in the league. One can imagine, therefore, that when a referee from a Northern Italian town arrived in their midst they were none too welcoming from the start; but as the score against them mounted their hostility grew with every goal. Finally, with Catanzaro 15–0 up, a Caserta player managed to get hold of the ball and kick it into the enemy goal. The fans went wild with delight – though not as wild as they became a few moments later when Signor Troni declared the player offside.

The Southern Italian temperament is fiery, and Troni had just ignited Caserta. As the fury of the crowd grew he fled to the dressing-room (with the whole Catanzaro team). The fans started hammering on the doors and the shouts took on a regular chanting sound, which gradually resolved itself into the syllables 'TRO – NI'. Eventually Troni and the Catanzaro side were released, but troops had to be called in and the rioting continued for two whole days.

Reinforcements were again called out in January 1974, when Catanzaro, in a 1–1 home game against Palermo, had two penalty kicks disallowed. The referee, a certain Signor Benedetti, was chased right through the town. Benedetti was fortunately a good runner, and had drawn some way ahead of his pursuers by the time the crowd reached the centre of town. Italian sporting folklore records that he nipped round a corner and dived into the open door of a restaurant. Finding an empty seat in an alcove, he slipped on a pair of dark glasses, summoned the waiter and ordered a meal of fish soup. Just as the soup arrived, the proprietor, a soccer fan himself who had just returned from the game, recognized Benedetti. With an angry *'Via di qua, mascalzone!'* he chased the referee out the back door, throwing the garlicky soup after him for good measure.

Benedetti, soaked and malodorous, took refuge in an empty house by forcing the window, and started to plot his revenge. Picking up the telephone he discovered that by some miracle it had not been cut off. He immediately rang the restaurant and told them the Catanzaro manager would be bringing the entire team to eat there in an hour's time. He then made another call to the Catanzaro manager, saying that he was the restaurant proprietor and was inviting the team to eat at the restaurant for one thousand lire a head, because as far as he was concerned they had won.

The team arrived, ravenous, ate and drank hugely, were presented with an enormous bill, and went berserk. The restaurant was wrecked and the manager of the Catanzaro team was sent to jail for assaulting the proprietor. Ten other arrests are reported in contemporary newspaper accounts.

THE GREAT TIMEKEEPER

Hemingway used to box regularly with Morley Callaghan at the American Club in Paris. One day in June 1929 Scott Fitzgerald came to watch and Ernest asked him to timekeep. They gave Scott a stopwatch and told him how to do it.

Nothing much happened during the first round, which seemed to disappoint Fitzgerald. Hemingway was supposed to be a fighter, and here he was, boxing cautiously. At the start of the next round Hemingway got a little careless, and Morley landed one on his mouth. Hemingway started to bleed, and the taste of blood seemed to infuriate him. All he cared for now was to land a heavy punch and he started dropping his guard and taking a lot of punishment. Some billiard players in the next room stopped their game and leaned on their cues, watching. Scott kept his thumb on the stopwatch, fascinated by the fight. Hemingway caught a glimpse of him out of the corner of his eye and leapt at Morley with a terrific punch, but Morley beat him to it and caught him right on the jaw. Spinning, he went down.

As he came to, blinking painfully at the light, what should he see but Scott wringing his hands. 'Oh, my God,' he was saying, 'I let the round go four minutes!'

'Christ!' yelled Hemingway, staggering to his feet. He stood there, staring at Fitzgerald. 'All right, Scott,' he growled, 'if you want to see me getting the shit knocked out of me, just say so. Only don't say you made a mistake!'

FINGER TROUBLE

One of the great characters of motor racing is Raymond 'Toto' Roche, General Secretary of the Automobile Club du Nord, a tubby, energetic Belgian who generally wears a baggy dark suit and a Homburg hat.

The start of the Belgian Grand Prix is notoriously apt to give trouble: space is limited and the heat is intense. With rank upon rank of Grand Prix cars revving their engines in the hot sun the timing has to be well co-ordinated to prevent the engines overheating between the 'start engines' signal and the 'off'. These high performance motors are not equipped with cooling fans, and if they run for more than about a minute while stationary they are apt to boil or burst into flames.

In 1957, Roche, standing in front of the roaring mass of cars, trying at the same time to keep order on the course, made a gesture at a photographer with his flag. The pent-up drivers interpreted it as the 'off' and roared away. Roche, sprinting as fast as his short legs would carry him in the mêlée, just avoided being flattened.

The following year disaster struck again. Everyone was kept waiting minute after minute in the scorching sun because one of the cars at the back failed to get its engine started, even after repeated pushes. Peter Collins's radiator was blowing out steam and the paint on his bonnet was blistering from the heat of the manifold by the time the second minute had ticked away. His engine became so hot that the oil pump could not generate enough pressure and he was forced to retire after only a few laps. The first two cars to finish both broke down at the end of the race, Mike Hawthorn's engine exploding spectacularly as he crossed the finishing line. He had to coast downhill to where Tony Brooks, the winner, was sitting in his overcooked Vanwall.

In 1959 Roche announced that he was instituting a new starting procedure which would put an end to these problems.

To make the 'off' signal absolutely unambiguous he was going to count down clearly with his fingers for the last ten seconds, so that everyone could see the time elapse. But when the moment came it was immediately apparent that he was having some difficulty grasping his flag in his right hand while counting on his left. He had failed to work out a method of holding the flag and counting at the same time, while still keeping the flag visible – and leaving enough fingers to count on. The count-down got as far as 'Ten . . . nine . . .' followed by a brief interval of frantic fumbling, whereupon Toto threw down the flag shouting 'Oh . . . GO!' and stood back – as all the cars piled into each other.

OLYMPIC WALKOVER

Four runners in the 400 metres race of the 1908 Olympic Games in London were coming round the last bend onto the final straight. The British runner Lieutenant Wyndham Halswelle challenged for the lead, but the US runner J. C. Carpenter moved out from the inside and blocked Halswelle's way, so that Halswelle had to move out across the track. As soon as he saw the American runner to all appearances fouling the sole British entry – all the others were American – Dr Badger, Vice President of the British Amateur Athletics Association, raced onto the track and ordered the judges to cut the tape. As a result of this dramatic intervention there was no winner and the race was declared void. Carpenter, though first to reach the finish, was disqualified and a rerun was ordered.

American rules about overtaking on the track were different from the British ones at that time, and it was not until four years later, when the International Amateur Athletic Federation was formed, that they were harmonized. It is therefore understandable that the American runners were angry at Carpenter's disqualification, and refused to take part in the rerun. There was also considerable animosity between the British hosts and the visiting Americans: the British were inclined to put on airs of superiority which the Americans felt to be totally unjustified, and there were so many accusations of partiality in judging that the British Olympic Association felt it necessary to publish a 60-page booklet, most of which was taken up with an explanation of the Halswelle affair.

The rerun of the 400 metres race was one of the oddest moments in Olympic history. The British judges were unable to persuade the remaining two American runners to participate but were none the less determined to carry on. Thus they found themselves presiding over a unique Olympic event: a one-man race. A photograph of Halswelle as he breasts the tape, arms raised, at the Shepherd's Bush stadium, shows a look of sublime assurance on his face – the look of the Edwardian Englishman for whom victory is pre-ordained.

THE FASTEST 100 YARDS IN HISTORY

In May 1955 a runner from Louisiana University ran the fastest hundred yards in history. The spectators cheered and the sprinter rejoiced. On that May day at Louisiana State's Tulane track he had achieved the unachievable. He had covered the distance in exactly 9.0 seconds.

The name of this glorious record-breaker will be known to comparatively few. (It was Billy Jones.) He will not be found in any of the record books. The reason for this is that when the track was remeasured by officials they discovered that it was only 90 yards long.

ODD ANGLES

Organizing an angling competition is a thankless task. If there are good catches there are sure to be arguments, and if nothing bites it is sure to be your fault.

A memorable competition was held on Boxing Day 1950 at Walton-on-the-Naze. The winner, Mr E. Curry of Bury St Edmunds, was rewarded with a 12lb turkey and a carton of cigarettes for landing a 9oz flounder. The other 158 competitors caught nothing at all.

At the National Ambulancemen's Championship held at Kidderminster in 1972 a keen sense of competition sustained the 200 anglers throughout the first five hours of intensive fishing. But no one caught anything. Towards the end of the day a passer-by paused to watch the proceedings and a wry grin spread over his face.

'Hey,' he called, 'has nobody told you? The Canal Authority drained that stretch of water three weeks ago: they've only just refilled it!'

Early in 1981 a fisheries scientist was doing some population samples along a canal in the Midlands and was interested to note an angler near the mouth of the coolant exit from a power station. The scientist asked whether that was a particularly good spot for catching fish, since the slightly warmer water ought, he imagined, to encourage a good growth of larvae and worms.

'Not any more,' came the reply. 'It used to be all right a couple of years ago, but it's all fished out now. Mind you, the whole canal is so poorly stocked that you'll as soon find fish here as anywhere. There's a big pike down there I've been after for a month or more – I know he's somewhere about but I doubt I'll catch him on a sunny day like this. And I wouldn't bother with that sampling machine of yours. Why, the chances of anything happening to swim into that contraption must be thousands to one against.'

Suppressing a desire to ask the angler what he was doing there himself in that case, the fisheries expert set up his machine a few yards down the bank. He started the motor (to much head-shaking from the angler) and inserted the electrodes into the water. He worked away busily for some time, then looked up to tell the angler his findings: the stretch of water he had measured contained an estimated population of several thousand trout, bream, perch and other fish. But the canal bank was empty, and there was no fisherman to be seen.

BLIND JUSTICE

Umpires, referees and linesmen are often accused by spectators and competitors alike of being blind, deaf, cross-eyed, or asleep, and one cold blustery June day at Wimbledon in 1964 this legend became historical fact. A lineswoman, Mrs Dorothy Cavis Brown, was found asleep by a ballboy on No. 3 Court. Segal and Graebner were leaving at the end of their match when there was a sudden outbreak of nudging and tittering among the crowd as they realized what had happened. Embodiment of a myth, Mrs Cavis Brown remarked between yawns: 'I have had a very exhausting time just lately.'

A BRILLIANT PROFESSIONAL CAREER

The sportsman whose amateur status is called into question does not always do badly at the hands of the authorities. The Swedish middle-distance runner Dan Waern contrived to get the best of both worlds for several years in the late Fifties.

Although Waern never achieved the world-wide fame of a Paavo Nurmi or an Arne Andersson, he nevertheless had a long record of unbeaten running in Scandinavia, and at home at any rate he was a superstar. His appearance would be guaranteed to draw the crowds, which endeared him to the Swedish Light Athletics League. For this reason they not only closed an eye to his appearances as disc-jockey and confectionery promoter, but took no notice whatever of his racing stable and a valuable country estate.

While the League were prepared to remain benignly aloof, waiting in the wings was a more hard-hearted gentleman: the taxman. With fiendish ingenuity, certain payments made by Stockholm Sports Clubs to D. Waern for 'appearances' were correlated against income tax declarations filed by the same man. Demands were issued. Scenting blood, the taxman started to sniff round other leading sporting figures. The papers got hold of the story and the League realized that something had to be done, so Waern was summoned before the disciplinary board.

The board then made a singularly courageous and unhypocritical declaration. Far from condemning the runner, they found that the payments were perfectly in order. They went on to state that amateurism in sport was nonsense anyway, and the whole concept should be abandoned.

This was too much for the International Amateur Athletic

Federation. After receiving very little co-operation from the Swedish authorities they decided, two years later, to suspend Dan Waern from international meetings.

The runner himself then made an announcement. The time had come, he said, for him to turn professional. Breathlessly the crowds awaited his first appearance, in an exhibition race of 1,000 metres against two teams of schoolboys and schoolgirls.

The event was quite a triumph for Waern. At least he managed to beat the schoolgirls – just. But the schoolboys beat him soundly, leaving the newly-fledged professional a full lap behind.

STONES' THROW

Among the most ingenious attempts at solving the problem of how to keep your amateur status without denting your payroll was that employed by Dwight Stones, the American world-record-holding high jumper and Olympic bronze medallist. He was invited in 1977 to appear on the television show 'Superstars' and, tempted by the $33,000 fee promised, took legal advice. He was told that he would not lose amateur status if the money was paid to a charitable institution or an organization set up for furthering sport. Accordingly Stones arranged for the money to be paid to the Desert Oasis Track Club.

The American Athletic Union, however, was suspicious and decided to investigate. It found that the Desert Oasis Track Club had only one member – Dwight Stones. They suspended him.

Stones then threatened a court action, since his legal position appeared sound. The American Athletic Union replied that they would reinstate him if he gave them the money earned by the 'Superstars' show. Realizing that his bluff had been called, Stones promised to withdraw the action and made a public apology for some unfavourable remarks he had made about the Union. He was reinstated.

SECOND CHANCES

One of the strangest of all Olympic results was the last-second win by the Soviet basketball team at Munich in 1972. The Americans had won every basketball final in the history of the Olympic Games, but this time the Russians were playing well and the Americans were finding them a tough side to beat. Indeed, right up until the last few seconds of the match the Soviets were marginally in the lead. The score was 49–48.

With six seconds to go the American guard Doug Collins stole the ball and raced to the basket, only to be knocked over by two Russians as he went up for his shot. A two-shot foul was called – with only three seconds left to play. Collins calmly sank both shots, giving the USA a 50–49 lead. The Russians put the ball into play and, with their coach screaming from the sidelines for time out, took a wild shot in desperation as the horn sounded. The Americans were leaping for joy when an official shouted that there was still another second of play.

To everyone's surprise all the officials present agreed that this was so. The players returned to the court, but in that extra second nothing happened to change the score. Just as the American players were beginning to relax and celebrate their victory (for the second time) *another* official intervened with the news that the clock had been wrongly set from the start: there were actually *three* seconds still left in the game.

For a third time the Soviets put the ball in play. This time a length-of-the-court pass found Aleksandr Belov, guarded by two Americans, right beneath the hoop. Belov knocked one guard over going up and the other coming down, leaving himself standing all alone with the easiest of shots as the horn sounded yet again – with the Russians the winners 51–50.

The American team, furious at the way things had turned out, left Munich without collecting their silver medal.

To those not familiar with basketball it must seem absurd that victory in this vital game between the world's two top countries could swing so wildly from one side to the other, and all in those last crucial seconds. It was certainly absurd that the timing mechanism could be so uncertain. Surely the officials could have arranged for an accurate clock.

But referees and officials of all sorts came in for a great deal of criticism at the Munich Games. There was for instance the much disputed decision over the boxing match between Valery Tregubov (USSR) and Reg Jones (USA): the Netherlands referee Jan Krom, whose casting vote gave the fight to Tregubov, was heavily criticized, and a few days later five referees were barred, sixteen judges warned, and two judges actually banned.

Americans know what a dramatic game basketball can be. On 29th April 1970 the New York Knicks were playing the Los Angeles Lakers when, just as in Munich, victory swung from one side to the other during the last few seconds. The game was tied 100–100. Then the New York forward Dave de Busschere hit a jump shot that put them ahead 102–100. There were no time-outs left for the Lakers, and it was assumed by practically everyone in the Los Angeles Forum that New York had won. Then in the last few seconds the Lakers' Wilt Chamberlain inbounded the ball in a casual-seeming way towards Jerry West. The New York guard hardly bothered to stop him as he dribbled from the far end of the court, but in the final tick of the clock West suddenly heaved the ball at the distant basket, from 70 feet away. Everyone in the arena held their breath as the ball soared through the air, descending in an arc which brought it, with incredible precision, exactly into that tiny 18-inch metal ring. As he saw it fall through the hoop de Busschere actually collapsed on the floor from shock. The arena exploded!

The Knicks won in the end, after a furious overtime struggle, but Jerry West's miraculous last-second shot is still talked of to this day.

For basketball, you need a good clock.

CHAMPIONS OF THE HURLED PUDDING

Although some sports officials are suspected of not being able to organize a drinks party in a brewery, they could hardly have done worse than the brewery-sponsored governing body of the World Haggis Hurling Association which organized the October 1980 World Championship.

Haggis hurling is not unlike shot-putting, with the difference that a shot, which weighs 16lbs, is heaved from the shoulder, while the 1½lb deep-frozen competition haggis is 'hurled'.

The finals of the 1980 competition were to be decided between teams from The Lade public house of Callander, Perthshire and the Hatter Bar, Marple, Manchester. After a summer of intensive hurling throughout the British Isles, the three-man Hatter Bar team achieved a cumulative throw of 326 feet 8 inches, which though considerably short of the previous world record team throw of 421 feet established in Birmingham, nevertheless qualified them for the final hurl-off against the team from Callander.

But when the lads from The Lade assembled at the hurling ground in Oban for the finals the Hatter Bar team were nowhere to be seen. Undeterred, the Scottish side went ahead, putting in a commendable performance with a 331 feet 2 inch team throw. Since their opponents had not materialized, they naturally assumed they would be granted the world title.

No such simple conclusion was reached by the officials organizing the event. For the Hatter Bar team had registered a claim for postponement with the World Controlling Body in Edinburgh. One of their members was on holiday, they explained. An objection was immediately lodged by The Lade, which contended that the non-appearance of the Hatter Bar hurlers invalidated their challenge. But the WHHA upheld the Hatter Bar claim, and then, in a dynamically original judgment, declared the two teams Joint World Champions.

There was an uproar. Adam Deans of the Scottish side declared: 'I feel we have stuck by the rules and the Association is being unfair. How can the English team be declared joint champions when they have not really thrown? I am very unhappy at what has happened.'

Robin Dunseath, President of the World Haggis Hurling Association, replied from headquarters in Edinburgh. He went straight to the point: 'There is a dispute over the rules,' he said. This was why, he explained, he had found it necessary to adjudicate. Presidents of World Sporting Bodies are there for precisely such emergencies.

All in all it had been a difficult season for haggis hurling. Right at the start of the season, at the world-famous hurling grounds at Bridge of Allan, Perthshire, an official measuring a hurl had been struck on the head by the haggis of the next hurler and knocked out.

5

Animals

Although animals are a necessary part of some sports, they may not always be pleased with their role. When they stray accidentally into the path of the sportsman a fiasco is almost certain to happen.

FIRST SHOOT YOUR LIE

Mrs Bobby Pritchard was enjoying a round of golf at Sinoia Country Club in what was then Rhodesia in 1952. After a good drive the ball bounded away somewhat off course into the rough, and Mrs Pritchard discovered that it had come to rest on the coils of a 10-foot python. She was at a loss as to her correct course of action. Should she play the stroke again with a fresh ball? Her scruples forbade this. Should she – horrible thought – attempt to hit the ball from the very back of the torpid reptile? What if she missed and sliced the python? All her instincts told her that it was better to let sleeping pythons lie.

She decided that it was a matter for the Club Secretary. This gentleman believed in a no-nonsense approach: 'First shoot the animal,' he decreed, 'then play your stroke.' And that is what she did.

Reported in *The Times*, the incident evoked a letter from P. G. Finch of Tunbridge Wells, who wrote to say that in Malaya in 1909 he had once played a ball from the back of a crocodile, citing as a witness a Mr Lachlan McLean. He admitted, however, that he too had thought it wiser to shoot the animal first.

DOUBLE TOP ADDER

An even more aggressive stance was adopted by the boys in the back room of a bar in remote Bindura, Northern Rhodesia in September 1952. On this occasion the rain was coming down in buckets outside and the boys were glad of the bar's shelter as well as its usual amenities. A resident, H. Shumbling, was taking a deep draught of some strengthening brew when out of the corner of his eye he spotted something calculated to give any drinker the shakes – a puff adder. It too was no doubt sheltering from the downpour but seemed to resent Shumbling's presence, regarding him with a coldly hostile eye and advancing menacingly across the floor.

The odds would have been on the puff adder had it not been for the presence of mind of the local darts champion, Colin Browne, who happened to have a dart in his hand. With a single flick of his wrist he pinned the beast, writhing, to the wooden floor.

There were celebrations all round, but the throw cost Browne his match. He had, after all, missed the board, and they take their darts very seriously indeed in Bindura.

UNSUNG HEROES

The history of sport is full of less menacing animals who strayed unwittingly onto the field of play and came to a sticky end. For example, in Lord's Cricket Museum a taxidermist has mounted the stuffed remains of a sparrow onto the ball which killed it, bowled by Jehangir Khan of Cambridge University to T. N. Pearce of the MCC. An unfortunate yellowhammer flew into the path of a golf ball struck on the second tee of Newton Green golf course at Sudbury by J. G. Powell in 1949. Little remained but a puff of yellow feathers. A butterfly was 'struck and killed' by a ball from C. J. Knott to Sir Derrick Bailey at Portsmouth in 1951 during a cricket match between Hampshire and Gloucestershire. And during a holiday cricket match at Ampfield near Southampton in August 1949 (Romsey were playing Chichester) a Romsey player hit a fine six out of the field which landed on a goose, causing fatal injuries. (In cricket a score of zero is known as a duck, from the round shape of a duck's egg, while in tennis the term 'love' derives from the French *l'oeuf*, or 'egg'. Should a six at cricket be named a goose to commemorate the Ampfield martyr?)

The first recorded instance of a bird intervening successfully during a game of cricket and materially assisting the side of its choice occurred during the sixth Test between England and Australia in Adelaide in 1981. A seagull heroically fielded a leg-glance from Keith Stackpole and saved England two runs. The gull was immediately treated for shock and a broken leg and, happily, recovered to field again (though it appears to have thought better of this idea).

Other animals have made brief and entertaining appearances throughout the history of sport, from the mouse which delighted spectators at the first Test Match at Edgbaston to the dog which managed to get into the No. 3 Court at Wimbledon while Australia's J. E. Sharpe was playing against J. W. Frost of the United States in 1962. A cockerel was released by a spectator on the field during the 1981 France vs. Holland World Cup qualifying game and spent the whole of the first half on the Parc des Princes pitch.

Famous cricketing dogs include the rather cowed-looking Alsatian which was chased by the South African player Dalton from the pitch at Manchester during the fourth Test in 1935, the mongrel Loxton shooed off the same pitch thirteen years later during the Australian Test, the one Goddard of Gloucestershire caught at the Oval in 1950 and the shaggy poodle England bowler John Lever rescued from the wicket area during the fifth and final Test against Australia in 1977.

An early mention of a cricketer's dog occurs in Richard Daft's account of George Parr, the Nottingham player and England captain during the middle of the nineteenth century. Parr was a martyr to gout in his later years and when Daft encountered him one hot summer's day he was stumbling along wearing a strange old bushwhacker's hat, holding an umbrella against the sun with one hand and a thick walking stick in the other. Attached to the top of the stick was the lead of his fox terrier, a constant companion.

'Why, Mr Parr,' exclaimed Daft jovially, 'I thought you were a blind man being led by a dog!'

The great sportsman looked at him and gruffly replied, 'I'd rather be led by a dog than a fool any day.'

GENUINE MING?

One of the most famous French horses of all time was Ming, owned by Count Gaston d'Audiffret-Pasquier. When Ming was being registered for the Cheltenham Championship Stakes in 1959 the Count unearthed some early identification notes on which there were some curious and inexplicable inconsistencies. It was stated, for instance, that Ming had 'a white blaze and three white stockings'. In fact, Ming was pure bay. The Count became perturbed: could this be his horse? Or rather, if Ming's markings were as described, was Ming *not* Ming?

The French 'Society of Encouragement for the Amelioration of Horse Breeds', backed up by the 'Society of French

Steeplechasers' took up the case. They probed into the animal's history and came up with an intriguing clue. Six years before Ming had shared a stable with a horse named Gaucho. Gaucho was a leisurely creature who had never won a race in his life. But his markings were pure Ming: the three white stockings and the blaze were indisputably just as described on Ming's identity papers. Was Gaucho really Ming and Ming Gaucho? In that case, who owned whom, and what should happen to the prize money 'Ming' had won? The mystery remains one of the most perplexing in the history of horse racing. No answer was ever found by French racing officials, and we are left with the uneasy feeling that what had been taken for many years as Ming was, after all, nothing but a twentieth-century fake.

WILY GROUSE

Grouse are wily birds, and any British grouse in its right mind is especially canny on the 12th of August. At the opening of the 1964 season guests on Lord Swinton's Yorkshire estate included the former British Prime Minister Harold Macmillan, but after four hours on the moors not a single bird had been conned into leaving its lair. One shot was eventually fired by Major David Jamieson at a bird which happened to be passing on an urgent errand. He missed. The only bird bagged during the entire day was taken by Major Jamieson's brother Jerry, who managed to smother one with his cap in the heather.

A PROPER EYEFULL

A cricket match was taking place in a small village in Gloucestershire in the middle of a particularly lush June. The grass was extremely long and contained more than the usual number of buttercups, celandines, daisies and other flora, to the evident delight of a dancing horde of cabbage whites and meadow blues. The sky was as blue as the butterflies and a herd of cows which had been grazing on the pitch until barely two hours before the start of the game were now standing pressed up against the fence at the far end of the field, looking on with mild curiosity at the funny humans who had invaded their favourite pasture.

The afternoon went by with dreamlike slowness. Very occasionally there would be the sound of a ball striking a bat, but nothing else disturbed the peace of the fielders standing dotted around the meadow, sleeves rolled up. More rarely still the batsmen would amble gently up and down the pitch and a fielder would be seen to walk a few paces one way or another, bend down and fumble for the ball in the long grass, then throw it in the general direction of the wicket. When this happened the umpire, a man named Martin with a ruddy face and a handlebar moustache, would take solemn note of the occurrence. After about an hour one of the batsmen – the visiting team were in first – became distracted by a couple of small boys attempting to launch a model glider from the roof of the converted cowshed pavilion, and failed to stop the ball which had been making its way towards him down the wicket. It hit the stumps and Martin declared him 'out'. A ragged round of applause went up from the few onlookers, including the umpire's wife Betty, a friend of hers, Sir Hugh Greene (who told me this story) and the two small boys (who were actually applauding their glider, now spiralling upwards in a summer thermal).

After a further interval a ball was bowled at the incoming batsman, who poked at it nervously. It described a slow arc and landed exactly in the middle of an enormous cowpat situated two feet in front of where Martin was standing. Martin, who had been glaring concentratedly down the pitch towards the batsman, received the entire cowpat smack in the face. Meanwhile the ball had vanished and the batsmen had started to run. They had had two runs and were starting on their third when the ball was thrown at the stumps. But when the appeal came Martin was in no condition to reply. How could he give a valid decision when he had been quite unable to see what had happened? Besides, his full attention was needed for the much more urgent task of wiping concentrated essence of cow out of his eye – not to mention his face, hair and handlebar moustache.

The two batsmen were leaning on their bats awaiting the umpire's decision. But all he would do was splutter and curse. Realizing they were technically speaking not yet out, they continued running. At this point the entire opposing team started to shout at the top of their voices and dance up and down. Betty Martin's youngest son then arrived at the double with a bucket of water for his father's face, tripped up, and spilled the contents over Martin, the bowler, and two fielders who had come to his aid.

THE WALLABY RULE

In the summer of 1949 the local fauna of Darwin, North Australia began to assert their prior rights to territory usurped by golfers. Hitherto those swift, frilly-necked lizards and goannas, otherwise known as 'monitors', had been content with occasionally snapping up balls lying on the edges of the jungle surrounding the course. But by 1948 the action of other animals became so intense that club members could no longer ignore it. 'Bomber' hawks started to swoop on the balls. Crocodiles, snakes and wallabies all made hostile forays. Halfway round the course in a giant pile of rubble waited a writhing contingent of huge snakes. Some sort of general offensive was evidently in preparation. Accordingly a new rule was adopted by the club: 'When a hawk, lizard, crocodile, snake or wallaby takes the ball, another shall be dropped.'

BEAR RULING

In the summer of 1961 Ocean Shores Golf Course, near Aberdeen, Washington was invaded by a large black bear. He lumbered about for some time on the fourth fairway, causing consternation among golfers, until he was eventually driven back into the woods by a helicopter.

In the aftermath officials posted a sign near the first tee headed 'Revised Summer Rules'. It contained the following additions: 'If a ball is picked up by a bear, player may replace and take one penalty stroke. If player gets the ball back from the bear, take automatic par for hole.'

DRACULA ON ICE

Ice hockey is difficult to organize in Britain, since there are so few ice skating rinks now in regular use. Even the old Christmas pantomimes on ice have become a rarity. My Canadian cousin Peter, who was a vigorous exponent of the game while at Oxford, told me of the difficulties he experienced in trying to get together a match against Cambridge. In the end they had to book the Queen's Rink in Bayswater for two o'clock in the morning – the only time it was free.

Consistently cold winters are a necessity if the game is to catch on at all widely. British winters, chilly and foggy though they may be, lack the necessary ferocity. Very cold conditions have their own drawbacks, though. An ice-hockey match between Portland and Denver scheduled by the Western Hockey League for January 1969 actually had to be cancelled because of cold weather: the carpark of the Portland Coliseum became unusable when it iced over.

Buffalo knows all about cold winters, and would no doubt have had an answer to Portland's problem. But towards the end of the season things grow less predictable. During a match in April 1975 between the Buffalo Sabres and the Montreal Canadiens ground mist made the rink almost invisible. As the moist air swirled down and condensed into steam over the ice the rink took on the look of a scene in an old horror movie. Padded and muffled figures blundered about, barely discernible through the miasma. At each end gaped the raw red mouths of the goals. Then a colony of bats, waking from their hibernation in the rafters of the stadium, started flitting about among the players. Don Luce and Craig Ramsey of the Sabres went for one with their sticks, and the game became a Transylvanian farce. Weird shrieks and yells rent the air, bats swooped, hockey sticks clashed, and four players not, like the bats, equipped with sonar, collided with each other and collapsed in a heap on the ice.

A GOOD DAY'S HUNTING

Bill Corriere of Easton, Pennsylvania went to hunt big game in Colorado, near the Little Snake River, where he brought down a big buck deer with a single shot. He had just begun to dress out the deer when a large elk came into sight. Corriere dispatched it with another shot. He went back to camp to find some horses to carry the game and upon his return found a bear nibbling at the deer. He promptly shot that too.

Arriving home to Easton, satisfied with his fantastic success, Bill spotted what looked like a partridge in a field near his house. Once more his aim was perfect. But the 'partridge' turned out to be his pet cat.

THE GREAT ALPINE WALKOVER

The worst steeplechase of all time was the December 1968 Prix des Alpes race. At the start there were eleven horses. Between them they managed to throw seven riders – three of them at the first jump. A couple of furlongs from the end, with just four horses left in the race, three took a wrong turning and left the course.

The remaining animal, Fanita, doggedly galloped on down the straight. But as the thudding of her companions' hooves grew fainter she began to feel that something was wrong. At the last jump she refused, throwing her rider and turning back to join the others. The jockey, pedestrian fellow, seemed to think that the race was still 'on', and chased down the course after Fanita, remounted, and coaxed her back up the straight and over the jump. Then, taking no chances, he dismounted and dragged her by the reins past the finishing line, 'winning' – literally – by a walkover.

MYTHICAL CROCODILES

During the Moscow Olympics of 1980 an athlete from Guinea Bissau refused to take part in the 3,000 metres steeplechase event. When asked why he would not run he explained that it was the water jump which worried him. You just don't jump into water in Guinea Bissau: there might be crocodiles.

TROPICAL JAWS

On 8th January 1969 at the Tropical Park race course in Florida, Hans II and his jockey actually did encounter an alligator on the first corner. They were overtaking another horse at the time and presumably put on even more speed after the unscheduled meeting. The alligator, a stray from the nearby swamp, appears to have escaped unhurt. The jockey, reflecting on his glimpse of the jaws of defeat at the end of the race, remarked: 'If I fall I'd better land on my feet and start running.'

INDIAN EMERGENCY

Microbes are very small animals with a special role to play in sporting fiascos: they cause dysentery. Ian Peebles, for example, describes an urgent incident which took place during an MCC tour of India under the captaincy of Lionel Tennyson.

Half the MCC team were down with the microscopic

complaint but one of the victims, Alf Gover, staunchly left his sick bed to make up the eleven for a match. Alf's first two overs were uneventful and during a third, as he started on his long, hustling run, only the most acute observer would have been alarmed at the tense expression on his face. It was when he shot past the crouching umpire and thundered down the pitch with the undelivered ball still in his hand that it became apparent to all assembled that something was amiss. The Indian batsman, fearing a personal assault, sprang smartly backward, but the flannelled giant sped past, looking neither right nor left. Past wicketkeeper, slips and fine leg in a flash he hurtled, up the pavilion steps – and in a cloud of dusty gravel he was gone.

Fine leg, after a moment's thought about his likely movements, followed Gover up the steps to the obvious place and rescued the undelivered ball from the bowler's convulsive grasp.

MONTEZUMA'S REVENGE

The mighty microbe was also at work at the soccer World Cup in Mexico in 1970, when England had one of the finest goalkeepers of all time on its side, Gordon Banks. Such was Banks's eminence – built on his exceptional combination of positional sense, level-headedness and acrobatic talent – that people joked in all seriousness about goals being 'as safe as the Banks of England'. He was awarded an OBE by a soccer-conscious Wilson government in January 1970 and when the English team travelled to Mexico later that year hopes were high for a repeat of their 1966 World Cup victory.

On 7th June in the first round England played Brazil, who also had a superstar: Pelé, the only footballer ever to stop a war (a truce was declared in Nigeria during the Biafran war so that both sides could watch the great man during his African visit). Brazil's forward line also boasted Tostao, Rivelino and Jairzinho – a truly formidable combination. But no one could get the ball past

Banks; his saves were heroic and even Pelé could hardly believe what he saw. Then, half an hour before the end, a combination of brilliant sideslipping and lightning footwork from Tostao to Pelé and then to Jairzinho gave not even Banks a chance, and secured Brazil's only goal.

A week later England was to play the imposing West German side, captained by Uwe Seeler and vaunting the unstoppable Gerdt 'der Bomber' Müller. But England had Bobby Moore as well as Banks, and had beaten Germany the last time, in the 1966 World Cup final. Spirits were high.

Then, the night before the match, Mexican microbes attacked. Banks, it was announced, was indisposed. He had Montezuma's Revenge.

Historians will recall that Cortés, with an army of 600 men, conquered several million Aztecs, under Montezuma, largely by unwittingly giving them smallpox, against which they had no immunity. As a legacy of that despicable act any 'gringo' who ventures south of Texas is attacked by millions of avenging microbes – or so the story goes. History is uncertain as to the exact organism that afflicted Banks but, whatever it was, it had a lot to answer for. If Banks had been in goal England probably would have beaten West Germany. Peter Bonetti, who replaced him, did splendidly (for the most part), but Banks was a lot better than splendid, and England did score two goals. If Pelé, Tostao, Jairzinho and Rivelino between them could only get one goal past Banks, would West Germany have got *three*?

Having lost the game, and with it England's hopes of getting into the semi-finals of the World Cup, a mood of gloom and defeatism settled over the British Isles. There was a General Election soon afterwards and Wilson was replaced by that well-known helmsman, Edward Heath. Banks's microbes should take the blame for that too: no doubt people felt that sailors would be less prone to attack. But, alas, politics failed once again to come to the aid of sport, or anything else for that matter, and England sank into a period of generalized fiasco.

LOCUST THREAT

Lord's Cricket Ground in London has had a number of narrow squeaks in its time. During the Second World War a V1 bomb landed on the pitch, but did not explode. One of the many curious incidents in the history of the ground was the threatened plague of locusts in 1970.

In a bizarre effort to further the anti-apartheid cause the biologist David Wilton Godberton of Colwyn Bay hatched a fiendish plot to destroy the pitch: 100,000 locusts were specially bred in the artificial warmth of light-bulbs in a chicken house, and the protesters threatened to unleash them if the 1970 South African cricketers' tour went ahead. In a graphic description of the coming wrath of the locust Wilton Godberton declared that the animals would make the sound of crackling flames as they devoured the grass at the rate of a hundredweight every twelve minutes. Having performed their task they would then expire heroically in the chill of the English May weather, so the gardens of St John's Wood nearby need have no cause for alarm. Luckily for everyone, however (including the locusts), the organizers of this extraordinary stunt announced, a few days after issuing their threat, that they had 'chickened out'.

KID VICIOUS

During the autumn of 1977 there was a spate of reports from the United States of aggression against the animal kingdom by young sportsmen.

Their methods were ruthless. On 3rd November the Denver-based American Humane Association asked the State Attorney General to investigate an incident in which a football coach had painted a chicken gold. The gold-painted fowl was apparently intended to represent a golden eagle, the symbol of a football team the coach was hoping to defeat. The players were then invited to treat the unfortunate bird like a football. They kicked it, squawking piteously, around the field until it expired.

A few weeks before, a school coach in Florida had been ordered to stop biting the heads off frogs during pre-game talks.

A BAR TO VICTORY

There have to be controls over the administration of drugs to horses. Athletes are not allowed them, and it would not be fair to allow to horses what is denied to humans.

Nevertheless horses, like human runners, are prone to temptation. At the Sean Memorial Handicap Hurdle at Worcester Park in 1979 the two-to-one favourite No Bombs won by eight lengths over Albion Prince. After the race the standard post-race urine test revealed trace amounts of two banned drugs: caffeine and theobromine. No Bombs was disqualified and first place was awarded to Albion Prince.

No Bombs' trainer, Mr Easterby, appealed, on the grounds that the so-called 'drugs', which were in any case present in minute amounts, had been administered unknowingly. It was later discovered that their source was a chocolate bar: before the race the gelding had snatched a Mars bar from the stable-boy's pocket. Mars bars contain small quantities of both caffeine and theobromine. When this evidence was produced, the Jockey Club agreed to waive the fine, but the result of the race remained unchanged.

ANIMAL POWER

One of the most disastrous ball games on record took place when a women's softball team named 'Animal Power' from Santa Rosa, California challenged the Budweiser Brewers in July 1979.

Animal Power was sponsored by a woman concerned with the conservation of endangered animals – hence their somewhat unusual name. One cannot help feeling that the efforts of these ladies might have been better spent actually *in* the field saving the wombats and wallabies from extinction, rather than *on* the field playing softball.

Before the game even started Animal Power's Debbie Young was hit on the face by a ball; nevertheless she bravely insisted on playing. Within the first few minutes of the game itself the pitcher, Tina Plyler, experienced knee trouble, and the game had to be interrupted while her knee was snapped back into its socket. The outfielders Ginny Harris and Jule Henex then collided with each other. Harris's shin was badly bruised, while Henex's ankle was fractured, and she had to be carried off. Henex was replaced by Bo Mari, who got on base the next inning only to collide with her rival catcher, shattering her elbow. She too was taken away to hospital.

Play was then resumed, but almost at once a ball popped out of Anna Young's glove and struck her teammate Dorene Baker on the cheek. At this point Tina Plyler began to get her knee trouble again. She also decided it was time she went home to feed her three-month-old daughter. The match was called off.

As the Animal Power team left the field the appropriate slogan printed on the backs of their uniforms took on an even greater meaning. It read: THE RIGHT TO SURVIVE.

WOMBLED

In 1946 a squirrel appeared on the No. 1 Court at Wimbledon while A. C. Van Swol was playing A. Punec of Yugoslavia in the opening round. It hopped around for a time, looking cute, to the great amusement of the spectators, who hoped no doubt that it was going to do a cartoon act by picking up one of the balls and holding it in its little paws like an outsized nut. Unfortunately it did nothing of the kind, and soon made its exit by climbing over the wire netting and making off in the direction of Wimbledon Common. I am told on good authority that it was a red squirrel. There are none of these left in the Wimbledon area now – they have all been eaten by Wombles.

6

The Inanimate

If there is anything more likely to cause a fiasco than the animal world, it is the inanimate. New gadgets and inventions are the bane of sport. Clothing is not to be relied upon.

GUCCI GLITTER

One of the tricks W. G. Grace used to employ when feeling mean towards a young cricketer was to call his attention to something in the sky, so that he would be blinded by the sun. It takes the eyes a surprisingly long time to recover their full powers after such treatment.

During a rugby match in Cornwall in 1970 (Cornwall were playing Surrey) the crowd used mirrors to distract the invading Surrey players. But how many people remember the cricket Test which was interrupted by a handbag?

The handbag belonged to Mrs Arthur Cowan, who was watching the second Test between England and Australia at Melbourne in 1959. The Australian player Colin McDonald, who was batting, protested that Mrs Cowan's handbag was shining in his eyes. Was it diamond-studded – or was it one of those very shiny white patent leather ones? The game was held up while Mrs Cowan was asked to place her bag in a less optically sensitive position.

BURSTING AND EXPLODING BALLS

Balls have burst on countless occasions during soccer matches – the two most notable perhaps being the two successive Cup Finals of 1946 (Charlton vs. Derby) and 1947 (Charlton vs. Burnley). During a match at Rio Prêto in Brazil in 1952 an enraged fan produced a rifle, tracked the ball and burst it in mid-flight as it was about to enter the home goal.

THE INFERNAL MACHINE

The nineteenth-century schoolmaster and cricketing enthusiast 'Felix', author of *Felix on the Bat*, was the inventor of a marvellous machine based on the principles of the Roman *catapulta* for serving nicely calculated leg-breaks and spins at batsmen in the nets. The 'bowling machine' was a dangerous contraption at best. Here is a contemporary account, from an 1841 edition of the *Wiltshire and Gloucestershire Standard*, of the Bowling Machine at Eton.

> 'The Rev. Mr Pickering, one of the masters at Eton, met with a serious accident last week. He and his friends had been using a machine called a "catapult", worked by powerful steel springs and intended to throw the ball with unerring aim towards the batter, when, by some mis-management the springs went off and the lever, striking Mr Pickering in the face with uncommon force, laid him prostrate. His right cheek was laid open from the upper lip to the extent of some inches. His life is reported to be out of danger.'

GETTING HIS BEARINGS

Another example of the dangers of technical innovation was seen in 1888 when Guy Nickalls won the Diamond Sculls at Henley. On the way to doing so he met W. Sweetman from the Isle of Wight in an early round.

Sweetman was sporting one of the patent new-fangled sliding seats which ran on bearings. Sliding seats, as a means of lengthening the stroke and bringing the leg muscles into full use, are now taken for granted in rowing, but the problems which attended them before they were perfected – a process which took many years – serve to remind the sportsman how difficult it is to get such inventions just right. On this occasion Sweetman's slide went disastrously wrong.

'His sculling was fitted for Southampton Water rather than the Thames,' wrote Nickalls.

He was referring to the naval firing range, for indeed, Nickalls suddenly found himself under fire.

'Shortly after the start, about halfway up from the island, I heard a bang, and a shower of shrapnel fell around me: the balls from his bearings.'

Generously, Nickalls offered Sweetman a new start, on condition that he provided himself with a less dangerous slide.

TRICKY BALLS TO HANDLE

There is a rule in cricket which prevents batsmen hitting the ball with their hands. The idea behind this ancient ruling, never applied at Lord's since J. Grundy playing for the MCC in 1857 manually deflected a ball from J. Wilsher, was presumably to prevent the game degenerating into a grass-field version of fives. But balls, inanimate though they may be, do some most peculiar things at times. For instance in June 1945 at Lord's a ball bowled by A. W. Roper, stopped dead by a turf-denting defensive stroke from G. O. Allen, rolled gently to the base of the stumps and came to rest. Without thinking, Allen bent to pick up the ball and threw it to Roper, who immediately appealed, imagining that the ball might have dislodged the bails. But to Roper's amazement the umpire, Fowler, who presumably thought this must have been Roper's intention in appealing, gave Allen 'out' for handling the ball.

W. G. Grace once used this rule to his advantage when batting for Gloucestershire against Surrey at Clifton in 1878. On this occasion the ball cunningly lodged itself in a fold of his ample shirt. Grace started running, and continued for several runs until a group of fielders rushed at him and dragged him to a halt.

'If I had removed the ball,' explained Grace, 'you would have given me out for handling the ball, so what did you expect me to do?' Three runs were eventually agreed upon. While he never broke the rules, said the old timers, it was marvellous what he could do with them.

It was marvellous too what he could do with a ball. In July 1876 in Hull, while scoring 126 for United South against United North, Grace hit a ball 37 miles. It landed in a railway truck and was found when the train next stopped – at Leeds.

SAILING BY

One evening in the early Fifties the comedian Ted Ray was enjoying a quiet round of golf with his friend Jack Wynne. As a golfer Wynne was noted for his phlegmatic approach to the game. He was a man who liked to chew on his pipe and survey the scene a good deal before venturing to disturb the ball. But on this occasion Ted became increasingly impatient as Jack seemed unable to find the right angle at the tee. His eye kept travelling from the flag to the tee and back again, and every time he looked he shifted his position.

'For Gawd's sake, 'it it!'

The cry came, not from Ted, but from the bargee, whose floating ensign Jack had mistaken for the flag at the fourth hole.

'How can a man be expected to play this game with bleeding sailors shouting at him?' was Jack's comment, as the barge glided slowly past along the canal bordering the links.

WINGED FEET

One of the extraordinary things about skiing is that simply by accelerating down a suitable slope one can leap into the air and cover an amazing distance, landing safely on one's skis. In 1934 a Yugoslav millionaire built a special ramp at Planica which enabled the ski-jumper to project himself into the air following an ideal trajectory, which immediately made it possible to jump far further than before. Skiers using this ramp found they were travelling so far through the air that they had time to adjust the angle of their bodies until they felt they were gliding. By 1948 the old world record of 87 metres had been raised to 120 metres by a jumper at Planica. But the Norwegians, who up until the 1956 Olympic Games had won all the gold medals for ski-jumping, refused to practise on the 'sensational' monster jumps, and scoffed at the idea that the skier had to shape himself into a living wing as he sped through the air. In view of all this talk about aerodynamics, they dubbed the new jumping style 'ski-flying', and the Norwegian gold medal-winner Birger Ruud declared that Norway should have nothing to do with artificially modified mountainsides. This had a disastrous effect on Norwegian ski-jumping, for techniques learned on the monster jumps were invaluable on the 70 metres Olympic jump as well. Norway failed to get another medal in Olympic ski-jumping until 1964, by which time the policy had been abandoned.

Another novel approach to ski-jumping was tried by the American skier Chuck Ryan, who in the winter of 1959 at the age of twenty-six established something of a record in this exhilarating sport. He pushed off from the top of the jump at

Duluth, Minnesota, sped down the track and soared into the blue. There he was, with the sky above, the ground below, and empty space all around as he hurtled down towards the runout area.

What made this jump so different from his many previous ones was that his skis, instead of being attached to his boots, were skittering down the ramp on their own.

He flew through the air for 150 feet, managing somehow to get his legs into a tobogganing position out in front of him, and touched down on the runout area, boots first, skidding a further 150 feet across the snow before coming to a halt. After this astonishing performance he picked himself up and walked away unhurt.

EXCEEDINGLY FINE CUT

There is a subtle 'one-upmanship' about clothes at Henley. Old rowing men turn out in fantastically striped blazers which they would never wear anywhere else, but which here, once a year, put to shame the ordinary man in his dull suit or 'casuals'. One cannot be too casual at Henley, however. There is more leeway than at Ascot, but the social distinctions are the more noticeable for that very reason. One can be made to feel quite inferior in the wrong clothes.

In the late Fifties the Australian Olympic sculler Stewart 'Sam' Mackenzie was drawn to row in the Diamond Sculls against an oarsman named R. D. Carver. It so happened that the race, which was scheduled for 3.45, left Mackenzie very little time to get to a rather smart wedding reception he had been invited to later that afternoon.

Mackenzie asked Carver's coach Derek Mays-Smith how Carver rated as an oarsman. 'You don't think I could ask him for a walkover, do you?'

Mays-Smith replied by suggesting that perhaps Mackenzie would like to retire himself – after all, he had already won the

Diamond once – he could go out on a high note. 'Carver,' he explained, 'is an exceedingly fine sculler.'

Mackenzie realized that he could not get out of the race, although he was going to have a terrible rush getting to his reception on time. He approached Arlett, the boatman at Leander boathouse, and asked him if, as a special favour, he would be so kind as to lift his boat out of the water for him and stow it away at the end of the race. He also asked if Arlett would mind if he left his morning coat and a towel behind the boathouse door, so that he could do a lightning change. The boatman, who knew Mackenzie well, said that of course that would be all right.

Mackenzie rowed mightily, leaving his opponent far behind. No sooner had he crossed the finishing line than he was leaping up the steps of the Leander boathouse. A few rapid flicks with the towel and on went the morning suit, not forgetting the top hat and stick. Placing the stick under one arm he was just in time to see Carver emerge from his boat. The resplendent Mackenzie strolled down towards the sweating, defeated sculler.

'Ah, Carver,' said Mackenzie, extracting his stick from under his arm and tucking his left thumb into his waistcoat pocket. 'Well done, old chap –' he tapped Carver lightly on the shoulder with his stick – 'an exceedingly fine paddle.'

SPLITTING IN STYLE

From time to time sportsmen take it into their heads to dress up in fancy clothes, an almost certain recipe for fiasco. In an elaborate celebration of the origins of the great game at Brunswick Terrace, Hove shortly after the last war, both teams appeared in full Regency costume. Brighton's Regency Club challenged, and in the end defeated, a team from the birthplace of cricket – Hambledon in Hampshire.

The Hambledon men looked quite dazzling in their jackets, knee breeches and stockings, whose colour scheme seemed to be selected from every portion of the spectrum: an awful warning of what might happen if the now traditional ruling about white flannels were ever relaxed. The Regency team were perhaps more stylish in their white suits, but their top hats in silver and gold or russet and green had a somewhat startling effect. Both teams used special bats, copies of the old bat in the Winchester College Museum. The umpires and scorers were even more fancily dressed in highly-coloured frock coats. One scorer was seen wielding a notched ash stick and knife, the other preferring the more up-to-date notebook and pencil.

The match was played for a stake of an eighteen-gallon barrel of liquid – said at first to be punch, but proving later in fact to contain English bitter. Bowling was under-arm, which may have accounted for the fact that at least a dozen balls were hit almost into the sea, falling short in Brunswick Terrace or on the beach. Since the players were following the 'New Articles of the Game as Settled and Revised at the Star and Garter, Pall Mall, on February 25th 1774 by a Committee of Noblemen and Gentlemen of Kent' – there were only four balls per over.

The final score was: Regency Club 183 for 10 wickets, declared; Hambledon 174 all out. In the words of *The Times* report of the match: 'Another unexpected detail of Regency cricket as applied to modern times was the number of players who suddenly discovered their breeches had split in a rather vital spot. This became so frequent an occurrence that players ceased to worry about it.' Or indeed, after the consumption of the contents of the eighteen-gallon barrel, about anything else.

TREACHEROUS ELASTIC

Trouser-failure is a malady that afflicts cricket players more than most – even when they are not dressed in eccentric costume like the Regency and Hambledon Clubs. There was for instance, the sudden splitting of Langley's trousers during the England vs. Australia Test in 1958; or the awful moment at the Oval in 1980 during the match between Surrey and Lancashire when the afflicted party was Lancashire wicket keeper G. Fowler.

Even more embarrassing misfortunes have occurred to women sports champions. At least two recorded instances are known of the ultimate disaster – loss of knickers – at Wimbledon. According to Roy McKelvie this happened first to Hazel Phillips on No. 10 Court, while John Legge was refereeing. When she asked Legge for permission to leave for a few minutes and put on another pair, he gave her a flat 'no'. It is strictly against the rules at Wimbledon for a player to leave the court during a match.

Word of what had happened soon spread among the press, who swarmed in from all directions. For once, Legge stretched the rules.

Margaret Court was playing on the Centre Court in 1975 when all the fastenings on her dress came undone. Simultaneously the elastic on her pants gave way. Luckily a WRAF steward was able to repair the damage with a handful of safety pins.

One of the best-selling photographs of the Seventies was of a girl tennis player who had evidently suffered the same misfortune. Although a posed shot, the fame it achieved shows how deeply the sporting fiasco is appreciated by the public.

TRAVESTY

As he pounded round the track at the Erith Athletic Ground one September day in 1971, the runner David Bedford, a European record holder in the 5,000 and 10,000 metres, heard through the ringing in his ears various confused shouts which he gradually realized were aimed at him. Bedford was running in the 5,000 metres race for the Shaftesbury Harriers in a Southern League interclub meeting. The day before, when he had set a national steeplechase record at the Crystal Palace, he had been given a standing ovation by the crowd.

There were only two laps to go. What could all the fuss be about? The loudspeaker system was out of action, so there had been a lot of shouting that afternoon. As he ran, to further confused shouts, he was hit in the face by a vest. 'Put it on!' yelled someone. Barely breaking stride he struggled out of his plain white vest into the one he had been thrown, which bore the name of the club he was running for, Shaftesbury Harriers.

In spite of this distraction Bedford won the race in 14 minutes 16 seconds. But he was disqualified. It is no use winning a race, it seems, if you have the wrong vest on, and particularly if, as the manager of the Chelmsford Club explained, you are seen to bare your back in front of spectators. They must indeed have been shocked – all eight of them!

Also shocking, in the eyes of the Women's Amateur Athletic Association, was the women's vest with a midriff ventilating panel sold by Ron Hill Sports in 1981. In a photograph of Lesley Watson, national marathon champion, it looks most becoming, though that may be due in part to the attractive Miss Watson. But the WAAA were worried, it seems, about what might happen if the vest became wet. One of their rules states that clothing 'must be made of a material that is not transparent, even when wet', and their secretary, Mrs Jill Lindsay, remarked: 'Even though dry you could see skin and bra straps clearly through the mesh.'

Dr Ron Hill, of Ron Hill Sports, who is himself a former European, Commonwealth and AAA marathon champion, was upset. He had already sold about 2,000 of the vests, and the British Amateur Athletic Board had signified its approval by ordering 30 for women due to compete in international events abroad in 1982. What is wrong with the British attitude to vests?

7
Fire

A sportsman on fire is the ultimate sporting fiasco.

FIRE AT THE SHOOT

Lord Wemyss and Lord de Grey (later Marquess of Ripon) were shooting on the Duke of Cleveland's moor at High Force one day in the 1880s. Both men were excellent shots, among the best in England, and there was a keen rivalry between them as to who could kill the most grouse. Both were on top of their form.

On the last drive Lord Wemyss drew the best position, and became extremely excited at the prospect of outdoing his rival. He was shooting away at such a rate that the black powder from his gun (this was in the days before smokeless cartridges) set fire to the butts behind him. But Wemyss was far too busy to let this bother him: a flaming butt didn't matter when beating Lord de Grey meant such a great deal. He made no attempt whatever to stamp out the fire and kept on shooting.

The turf was dry and the fire from the smouldering butt spread quickly in the stiff breeze. Eventually even Wemyss was driven out, but not before he had outshot de Grey and could, at last, lay claim to being England's top game shot.

The flames, meanwhile, spread over the moor and the entire workforce on the estate had to be employed in bringing buckets of water up from the valley in a vain effort to stop it. It burned on for a fortnight.

FIRE IN THE HAND

Sunday 1st September 1968 was a memorable day for Barcelona: the runner Gregorio Rojo was carrying the Olympic torch into Spain. Flags were flying, music sounding, and a large, enthusiastic crowd gathered along the city's main avenue. The police were working hard to keep them back, to leave the way open for the arrival of the athlete and his important burden. A joyful cheer went up as Rojo, accompanied by the runner Miguel Mariana, at last came into sight, holding the burning beacon high. Suddenly there was a roar, and a blinding sheet of flame. Athletes and crowd alike covered their faces in dismay. The Olympic torch thudded to the ground. It had exploded.

1968 was a bad year altogether for the Olympic torch.

All Olympic torches are lit by hallowed tradition at Olympia in Greece, from a flame kindled by the sun's rays (although electronic transmission of the flame by satellite to another continent is now considered valid). During the process of carrying the 1968 torch to Grenoble in France, on a deliberately circuitous 4,500-mile journey, it went out 28 times. Spares, all kindled in the approved fashion, had to be called upon. In Corsica some bandits tried to steal the flame and hold it to ransom but gave up the idea, cursing, when they were told that there were four more back-up torches all on their way to the same destination.

In 1976 the Montreal Olympic torch was extinguished during one of the heavy rains that marred the Games, and was quietly re-lit by a stadium custodian using a rolled-up newspaper. Dismayed officials, upset at this break with tradition, insisted on a proper re-lighting ceremony, even though no one had actually seen it go out in the first place and it had, of course, to be extinguished again before being rekindled.

MOSES LIVES

The golf course at Carnoustie lies alongside the North Sea just east of Dundee. During the summer of 1973 there was something of a drought in eastern Scotland, and the whole area took on a rather parched appearance. Mr F. Morton of Chessington, Surrey was visiting Carnoustie for a golfing holiday and had just played from the 16th tee when a clump of bushes near the green suddenly and spontaneously burst into flame.

Mr Morton, a determined golfer, was not going to have his game interrupted by anything so trivial as a bit of smouldering foliage. He and his friends continued their game right up to the green, though at this point things became rather difficult: the right-hand side of the green had become a furnace. Refusing to be put off by this they simply invented a new rule whereby any ball entering the overheated and unplayable right half of the green was to be replaced by another ball, exactly the same distance away from the flag, on the left half. Happily, they putted away. In the background groundsmen were struggling manfully to put out the blaze, and as Mr Morton sank his final putt he could hear the siren of an approaching fire engine. He managed it just in time, and got his par three for the hole.

'I looked at the rules afterwards,' he said, 'to see if there was anything about balls unplayable due to fire hazard, but I couldn't find anything.'

MATCH PLAY

The landscape and villages of the New Forest have a unique charm which is well described by the novelist James Wright in his books *The Devil's Parole* and *Spitfire Summer*. James Wright is a genial, untidy man with a pipe generally between his lips, and is well known in the literary world, having worked for many years as fiction editor in a major firm of publishers. His great passion in life, apart from books and music, is cricket, which he first played as a boy in the wartime years on the sandy New Forest turf.

Just after the war, in that first summer of peace, James was asked to play in a match at the village of Burley. Before the match he remembers having to roll up his sleeves and stuff his smoking kit into his pocket in order to manhandle some heavy iron hurdles off the pitch. These hurdles interlock to form a fence which protects the pitch, when not in use, against the depredations of New Forest ponies, not to mention cyclists and small boys. In order not to damage the thin topsoil of the New Forest they have to be carried, not dragged, to the edge of the field—a somewhat exhausting process.

It was a peaceful afternoon. The sun shone, the clouds were fat and lazy, the skies were full not of Spitfires but of skylarks, and if you can envisage a wicket keeper who is not only relaxed but on the very borders of a daydream you can imagine just how

it was for James—when the bomb went off. It was an incendiary bomb, and it was in his right-hand trouser pocket. Leaping up and down, tearing at his flaming trousers with his clumsy wicket-keeper's gloves and yelling for help at the top of his voice, James Wright had suddenly become the busiest man in England. The other players gathered round, tore the smoking material from his legs and escorted him trouserless to the pavilion to dress his wounds.

The incendiary bomb was of course a box of Swan Vestas ignited by the impact of a cricket ball.

Exactly the same thing happened in June 1969 to Mike Barnard, playing for the Bournemouth Wayfarers who were visiting the Marnhull team in Dorset. Barnard was batting when his incendiary bomb went off, and he is reported to have leaped from the crease with a yell, making for cover point. Once again a ring was formed around the smouldering cricketer and his scorched white flannels were ripped from his body. Ken Bishop, the umpire, gave him 'out' when he left the crease, but was afterwards prevailed upon to reverse his decision.

AT THE SALUTE

The British Tornado Class yacht entered for the 1976 Olympic Games at Montreal struck a submerged log during the racing. Extensive repairs were needed which increased her weight, added various bumps to her hull, and gave her something of a 'patchwork quilt' appearance. Her performance also deteriorated and she did not do well in subsequent races. At the end of the Games her crew had to decide what to do with her. They did not want the expense of shipping the damaged yacht back to England. They could not just leave her there. They could not sell her, since she had been imported on a special temporary permit to take part in the Games. Anyway, in her altered condition she would not have fetched very much.

Thus it was that spectators witnessed a memorable spectacle in the race area after the last race was over. There she floated, her sails flapping gently, headed into wind, while her crew of two busied themselves over something which appeared to require all their attention. Suddenly a wisp of smoke was seen to rise from the hull, and soon flames spread forward throughout the boat, while her crew stood stiffly in the stern at the salute, with yachting caps on their heads. With a hiss and a cloud of steam, she sank beneath the waves.

8

Weather and the Field of Play

'If people will insist on playing games in dense fog, at the North Pole or on the moon, what can they expect?'

– Veteran sports columnist

WHEN THE GOING WAS ROUGH

In the early years of cycling in Western Australia races were held annually on the grounds of the Western Australia Cricket Association. The ground was hard and chalky, and the chalk itself was composed of ill-digested fragments of sharp seashells, which after a rainstorm would cut tyres to shreds, forcing the cyclists to retire punctured – to the accompaniment of jeers from the cricketers. Other hazards facing the intrepid cyclists were the deadly 'double gees' – the spiny fruits of a weed which would be blown onto the track, with a similarly deflationary effect. At Albany on one occasion an unexpectedly high tide coming in fast over the flat sea-front had the cyclists pedalling for their lives.

These were the sort of conditions which made Australian cyclists tough. An unknown poet (or was it Banjo Paterson hiding behind the 'anon.'?) composed a song to celebrate the 1897 Austral cycle race, to the tune of 'After the ball is over'. This is a sample verse:

> After the Austral's over,
> After the track is clear,
> Straighten my nose and shoulders –
> Help them to find my ear.

Cut to pieces, no doubt, on the shells, or impaled in a tuft of double gees.

THE DAY THE BALLOON WENT UP

One autumn day in Belfast in 1886 a crowd of lively Irishmen, a dogged German, a monster balloon and a great deal of hydrogen were all assembled under a stormy sky. The *Ulster Observer*, reporting the incident, quite irrationally exonerates the balloonist in charge of the party, a Mr Coxwell, from all blame. He had given the passengers perfectly clear instructions as to what they should do when the balloon approached the ground at the end of the voyage: they were to sit down facing each other and prepare for some heavy shocks. They were then to leave the car one at a time, each seize hold of a loop of the rope girdle, and remain in position until the envelope was quite empty.

What could be clearer? But they did nothing of the sort:

> 'They behaved in the wildest manner, completely losing their self-control. Seizing the valve rope themselves, they tore it away from its attachment, the stronger pushing back the weaker, and refusing to lend help when they had got out. In consequence of this the car, relieved of their weight, tore away from the grasp of Mr Coxwell and those who still clung to it, and rose above the trees, with Mr Runge and one other passenger, Mr Halferty, alone within.'

Before long, the balloon started to descend again. The two remaining men called out to some farm labourers, who stood there laughing and chewing straws. The anchor then caught and the car slammed into the ground, expelling Mr Halferty and leaving the tenacious Herr Runge inside. Thus lightened, the balloon rose yet again into the air. Herr Runge was alone. In his own words:

> 'The balloon moved on, very soon, in a horizontal direction straight to the sea, which we were then rapidly nearing.

Coming to a farm, I shouted to the people standing there. Some women, with their quick humane instincts, were the first to perceive my danger . . . The anchor stuck in a willow tree. I shouted out to the people below to secure the cable and anchor by ropes, which they did. The evening was now beautifully still, the breeze had died away, and the balloon was swinging calmly at its moorings above the farmhouse. One of the men asked me whether I had a rope with me, and how I intended to get out.'

Before Runge could answer the wind returned and snatched him away, anchor swinging wildly. A fourth touchdown at another farm resulted in the loss of the anchor cable, and escape was only effected by a desperate plunge into a hawthorn hedge which ran along the top of a cliff. And there Herr Runge lay, struggling with the prickles, watching the balloon drift away into the twilight over the Irish Sea.

SWIMMING FOR DEAR LIFE

During the first modern Olympic Games, organized by Baron de Coubertin and held in Athens in 1896, the aim was to keep everything in the strict classical tradition. Contestants in the swimming events were simply taken out to sea the requisite distance in a boat, and expected to dive overboard and swim back to shore.

However much this idea might have appealed to poets and students of Homer, it was far from foolproof. Phaleron, near the bay of Piraeus, was hit by an April squall, and contestants in the 1200 metres event found themselves contending with 12-foot waves. To make matters worse the water was icy cold – indeed the winner Alfred Hajos may well have owed his victory to having taken the precaution of smearing himself with grease beforehand.

Valiantly the swimmers struggled with the breakers, and

gradually their Olympic zeal was overtaken by a more immediate concern: 'My will to live finally overcame my desire to win,' said Hajos afterwards.

Although no one was actually drowned, three-quarters of the shivering, exhausted entrants had to be rescued from the heaving water by lifeboat.

In recent years we have come to take the very high standard of perfection in the Olympic pool as the natural order of things: the huge 50m × 21m expanse of water heated to an even temperature of exactly 25°C, the special gutters to cut wave action, the eight lanes divided by those familiar red and white plastic floats . . . Such is our complacency that a *deliberate* lack of perfection can also cause a fiasco, albeit of a small kind.

The separate Olympic diving pool is five metres deep, and has a lift to take competitors to the diving platform. The water is *artificially stirred* to break up the surface.

During the Rome Olympics a BBC commentator was watching Brian Phelps preparing for the handbalance dive from the 10 metre board when another diver got into the lift. The action of the lift naturally made the board shudder and Phelps paused before his dive, waiting for the vibrations to stop. The commentator, observing this, observed sagely to his listening audience: 'Here's Phelps now, standing on the end of the board, just waiting for the water to settle before he dives.'

A GRACEFUL EUPHEMISM

There is nothing more treacherous than a cricket pitch slippery after a light sprinkling of rain. The Sussex Martlets were playing the Duke of Norfolk's team at Arundel under such conditions, and the Duke himself was in to bat at the non-striker's end. The other batsman, thinking it would be polite to give the Duke the chance, pushed the ball to cover and shouted, 'Come on, your Grace.' The Duke started off down the slippery pitch and the inevitable happened: over he went, flat on his face. Cover point threw the ball in to the wicket keeper, who whipped off the bails and appealed.

The umpire at this match was none other than the Duke's butler, Meadows, who had been summoned at the last minute from his pantry when no one else could be found. Conflicting emotions warring in his breast, Meadows looked daggers at the crowd, stuck out his chest, and holding his coat lapels in the way butlers do pronounced his verdict: 'His Grace is not in.'

TOO MUCH MOCHA

It is bad enough for sportsmen to have to fight their way through blizzards and gales, but what can an amateur team do when the hostile climate it faces is not meteorological but financial?

The worst financial climate of this century prevailed at the time of the 1932 Olympic Games at Los Angeles. Wall Street had seen the famous crash of 1929 and the world was in the grip of harsh depression. Although the Americans made every possible effort to help athletes competing in the Games many teams were desperately short of money and found it very hard to attend. The

Brazilian team pleaded in vain with their government for funds. But if the Brazilian government were short of money, the one thing they were not short of was coffee: the Brazilian Olympic Committee persuaded the government to lend them a ship and give them 50,000 bags of the bean to pay for their expenses. The plan was to sell the coffee on the journey between Rio and Los Angeles.

The problem was that the world had too much coffee already. Wherever they docked the answer was the same: prices were at rock bottom, and no one wanted any more of the stuff. Eventually the ship berthed at Los Angeles but only 24 members of the team had enough money to land. The others all put to sea again, setting off once more in the hope of selling the coffee somewhere, so that they could raise enough to get to the Games.

They had no luck and were barely able to pay for the fuel to get back to Los Angeles – just in time to take the 24 athletes, none of whom had won a medal, back home to Brazil.

GOLFING GALES

The Royal St George's Golf Club at Sandwich is notorious for its gales. One of the worst of these occurred on the third day of the 1938 Open Championship, which was won by R. A. Whitcombe. The style of the day was set when the wind tore the large Traders' Marquee to shreds, and scattered its contents over the landscape. Balls were blown 'like rooks about the skies'. One lucky golfer with the wind behind him drove 380 yards straight onto the eleventh green and was down in two. But crosswind play was totally erratic, and one player after another despaired as efforts to drive upwind into the teeth of the storm became increasingly useless. The balls just kept coming back.

A similar gale was blowing at Sandwich on the second day of the 1899 Open, which was won by the professional Harry Vardon. The evening after the match Vardon was relaxing in the clubhouse with Jimmie Braid and J. H. Taylor, when one of the club's newer and more timid members – a teetotaller – was seen advancing towards the bar and demanding brandy. Catching Vardon's eye he explained that he had been driving at the fourth hole when the wind caught his ball and knocked it into a nearby road – King's Avenue. It hit a delivery boy on a bicycle and knocked him into the ditch, an oncoming coach swerved to avoid him, crashed into a wall and burst into flames.

'And all because of my wretched ball: my God, what should I do?'

'Try adjusting the thumb of your left hand a little to the right when you address the ball,' was Vardon's laconic reply.

RAIN STOPS PLAY

Rain very often holds up play in outdoor sports such as cricket and tennis. But *table* tennis? Impossible, because the game is played indoors. Nevertheless, a world championship table tennis match was once postponed because of a sudden rainstorm.

The setting was Calcutta, 1975, in a newly-built stadium at the Eden Park Cricket Ground. Security before the event had been less than stringent and thieves had stolen all the toilets, the plumbing and the lead from the roof. Then there was a torrential downpour, and most of it came through the leadless ceiling. Eventually the rain let up and it was decided to go ahead with the first round, but when the opening ceremony finally got under way the band was missing.

The over-zealous thieves had stolen their tickets and they had been refused admission.

Weather also interfered with table tennis during the World Championships in Munich in 1969, when it was so cold that the balls froze solid and wouldn't bounce. The tables also grew very 'slow' from absorbing moisture. It was no surprise, in these conditions, when the 'slow' player, Eberhard Scholer, won easily.

Eventually hot-air driers had to be brought in to liven things up.

A LOST EAGLE

When you are hunting in vain for your lost golf ball or, like Alletson at Hove Cricket Ground (see p. 24), trying to prise the last ball out of the woodwork of the pavilion, spare a thought for a sporting pioneer who went searching in the backwoods of Eagle Harbor, California and was never seen again.

The name of Julius T. Nachazel is revered by frisbee throwers the world over. The Julius T. Nachazel Cup commemorates this great thrower and searcher, who never gave up, and may, for all we know, still be camped out somewhere in the wilds, grizzled and bearded, doggedly following the trail of the lost frisbee. The Cup itself, a splendid contraption consisting of one outsize galvanized tomato tin welded to a beer can and resting upon the lid of a container which once held coffee, is awarded to the team champion every year.

KNEE-DEEP IN SUGAR

The Carreras Jamaican 1000 Rally crosses and recrosses Jamaica in a complex pattern which makes full use of the island's varied landscape of bananas, sugar cane plantations and white sand. During the 1969 rally, however, one special stage of the 1,000-mile route had to be cancelled and others were made almost impassable when a sudden violent thunderstorm caused flash flooding in many areas, including the capital, Kingston. One intrepid rally driver, his enthusiasm quite undampened, employed a local resident to sit on the bonnet of his car and direct him through the shallowest parts of the flooded roads.

The scheme worked well until, negotiating a sugar cane plantation in this fashion, they reached the deeper water of an intersecting main road. Here the driver was forced to abandon his car to seek help, while the Jamaican 'pilot' remained behind, standing faithfully at his post on the bonnet of the car, which was projecting into the crossroad. The minutes passed and the flood waters continued to rise. Eventually the bonnet was completely submerged: the Jamaican's feet and then his legs began to disappear.

It was then that fiasco struck. Another rally car was approaching at speed down the main road towards the flooded area. The Jamaican gestured a frantic warning but the driver,

observing what he took to be a spectator standing at the side of the road, with the water barely up to his knees and waving in what seemed to be an encouraging manner, stepped on his accelerator and plunged on into the flood.

Only when the car lurched to a very splashy halt did he become aware of the existence of the other vehicle: just a few inches of its roof were now visible, and these had been hidden from sight by the tall sugar cane. The Jamaican was still standing on the submerged bonnet, wearing a somewhat perplexed expression, with the rising waters swirling around his knees.

THE ULTIMATE FIELD

If sporting fiascos are allowed to have any heroes, one of them must undoubtedly be Commodore O. C. S. Robertson (retired) of the Canadian Navy. Commodore Robertson was aboard the nuclear submarine USS *Seadragon* during its historic voyage through the northwest passage to the North Pole.

For days the submarine forged her pioneering way under the polar cap, surfacing through the ice from time to time to make observations. Finally they reached the Pole, and Robertson emerged with a number of officers to view the frozen waters. Before very long the idea came into his head that what everyone needed was some exercise and recreation, so he organized a baseball game. Having located the exact position of the North Pole with some care, he decided that this spot should be designated home plate. First base was thus in the Eastern hemisphere, third base in the Western, and the international dateline ran between home plate and first. The delightful consequence of this was that it took a day for the ball to travel from home to first.

The game got under way and the sailors began to enjoy the experience of being the first sportsmen to play a game literally on top of the world. After all, until Buzz Aldrin's record-breaking golf drive on the surface of the moon, they could lay claim to the most outlandish sportsground in history.

It was Sunday on *Seadragon*'s side of the dateline, so they looked forward to a full morning's play. Then suddenly the fun was stopped short and the game ended by an urgent signal from the submarine: Commodore Robertson was wanted at once by the communications officer. Robertson, panting, reached the submarine and picked up the hot line.

'Hullo,' he barked anxiously.

'Oh, hullo dear,' replied his wife's far-away voice. 'I hope I'm not interrupting anything, but it *is* rather vital. What on earth happened to the spare car keys?'

LORD'S HAILED

Towards the end of June 1968, in the middle of the 200th Test between England and Australia, Lord's Cricket Ground received a bizarre telephone call from a Mrs Doris Munday, who wanted to know whether the pitch was covered in hailstones. As a matter of fact it was; there had just been a violent thunderstorm. Well, Mrs Munday announced, she was responsible. And until the Australians paid up the money she was owed they could expect more.

Mrs Munday had, it appeared, an uncanny gift for causing hail to fall, first discovered by a hypnotist friend several years before. Since then she had been breaking droughts the world over, unleashing the odd freak storm where the mood took her and, when in a more benign spirit, making sure the weather kept fine for friends' holidays. But she had a grudge against the Australians.

Three years before the Lord's incident Mrs Munday had been asked to break a seven-year drought in Central Australia, on the promise that a collection would be made for her if she succeeded. But some Aborigines were also consulted, and when the rains came they were given the credit. Mrs Munday didn't get her money. This rankled, and she hit upon the idea of attacking Australian sport in revenge, choosing the Brisbane Test of 1966 as her first target. (With, cricket historians will agree, every appearance of success.) And she had, as she herself put it, been bashing them ever since.

Had Mrs Munday prolonged the spell of bad weather at Lord's it could indeed have been unfortunate for the Australians. But perhaps she felt a further contribution on her part was not necessary: England got Australia out for 78 in their first innings.

STORMY ENCOUNTER

Japan and China enjoy a relationship which tends to be tense, although diplomatic efforts to improve matters by cultural and sporting exchanges are frequently made. In September 1978, for example, Japan invited China to an athletic meeting on the island of Kyushu in southern Japan. But an equally tense situation quickly blew up over the weather.

The meeting was opened on 15th September, despite warning reports of an impending typhoon. The Japanese were anxious, but felt that if they postponed the event the Chinese would suspect some veiled insult: given the diplomatic delicacy of the occasion, oriental courtesy and hospitality had to take precedence over caution. Their poise began to falter, however, as things got under way amid the rapidly rising wind. Soon

athletes were seen to be working hard to stay in one place in the violent gusts. Finally composure cracked altogether and the meet was cancelled when two Sumo wrestlers, in their loose traditional costumes, were lifted bodily by the wind and thrown several yards towards the stadium entrance.

SEA TRIALS

The trials for the United Kingdom yachts competing in the America's Cup in May 1964 were among the most futile in the history of competitive sailing. Problems began for Owen Aisher's *Kurrewa* and J. A. G. Boyden's *Sovereign* when they were unable to find the Committee boat in the fog. After half an hour's search in poor visibility it was located, unanchored, four miles from its designated point. Then the weather mark evaporated in the mist. At any rate it was not in sight after what seemed like hours of difficult sailing in the windless conditions. A trawler suddenly materialized out of the not-so-thin air and bore down upon the helpless *Kurrewa* with relentless momentum; she only saved herself at the last moment by launching her tender and sending an ambassador to persuade the trawler to alter course.

Finally a breeze, of sorts, arrived, and *Sovereign* decided that if they hadn't seen the weather mark by now they never would: they must have overshot it. *Kurrewa*'s crew were then confronted by *Sovereign*, spinnaker bellying out, sailing in the opposite direction. Deciding that *Sovereign* must know something they didn't, *Kurrewa* altered course and gave chase, sailing splendidly along before the wind. All of a sudden something massive and cliff-shaped loomed out of the murk. Realizing that the spring-tides must have carried them on to the Isle of Wight, both yachts rapidly lowered their spinnakers and again reversed direction.

And so they sailed onward for many a day and a night – well, two and a half hours past the start at least – and all about them the sea was an empty and lifeless expanse. At this point it was universally deemed that the trials were over, and they had better do some fairly smart navigation if they were ever to see Cowes again.

Both yachts made it back to civilization, to the immense relief of all, but the episode was not a promising one for the America's Cup race itself. In the event the American boat *Constellation* beat *Sovereign* by 20 minutes 24 seconds – the largest margin since *Mayflower* beat *Galatea* in 1886.

A BAT OUT OF HELL

The Black Mountains of Wales have a magnificent lowering look. Their grassy sides, broken by granite crags, are vast, treeless and precipitous. Farmers tell of strange happenings on their sinister windswept heights – of sheep which vanish into oozing crevasses and of eerie cries at dead of night. The Baskerville family, which lived for generations at Clyro in the Wye valley below the Black Mountains, have long grown weary of having their name linked with the monstrous hellhound tracked down by Sherlock Holmes in the Conan Doyle story – though the author tactfully changed the story's location to Dartmoor to avoid just such an association. From time to time the carcasses of lambs and sheep are still found on the moors, bleeding from the claws of some fearsome predator, and an eagle or a wild dog is blamed.

One blustery March day in 1981 a hang-glider pilot was soaring high above Hay Bluff, not five miles from Clyro, seat of the Baskervilles. The previous two days had been windless, and hang-gliding enthusiasts had sat impatiently on the heights, watching their cigarette smoke drift straight up into the motionless sky, knowing that any attempt at flight would merely result in a rapid descent to the valley floor. Now, at the end of the weekend, on Sunday afternoon, a wind had sprung up, though the frontal system that brought it had a menacing look, and was bringing squalls of rain and violent gusts as it sped over the western hills towards the Beacons. The temptation to fly after days of frustration was too great for one intrepid pilot and he launched himself off over the ridge into the teeth of the gathering storm. He was riding hundreds of feet over the western face of the plateau, the black clouds were scudding overhead, and a deep chill was in the air as the first raindrops splattered into his helmeted face. The fabric-covered sail of his machine had started to luff as his speed built up in the rough air, and visibility was getting poor as the cloud cover increased. The ground receded below him and he was alone with the turbulent sky.

Or was he alone? Out of the corner of one eye he became aware of something large, dark and web-winged, riding up into the storm alongside him. As he turned he blinked incredulously, and nearly lost control of his wings. This was no hang-glider. It had a long pointed beak which turned from side to side, hunting into the wind. Its eye was yellow and its head bore a flaming crest. It had red claws on its wings, and scraggy fur on its horrible ribbed abdomen. In no mood to linger and find out what it was the hang-glider banked sharply, lost height as fast as he could, and made for the open stretch of road on the plateau at the foot of the Bluff.

Far below a small and chilly group stood on the Bluff's windswept edge. One of them held a radio transmitter, another wielded a Nikon with a telescopic lens. Mike Marten of the Science Photo Library was urging the photographer to get a picture before the light went altogether. This was an opportunity that might never come again.

I too was most anxious to come back with a good set of photographs. For it must now be explained that the monstrous winged apparition was not the Bat of the Baskervilles or a phantom out of a Welsh time-warp, but a life-size radio-controlled model of the giant prehistoric flying dinosaur *Pteranodon ingens,* which I had built at the cost of much time and labour for a BBC television programme.

The BBC wanted some action photographs. I had not calculated the terrorizing effect my model might have on hang-glider pilots, indeed I was only too keen to direct it as far away as possible from the danger of a mid-air collision, in which its fragile fibreglass and balsawood structure would be bound to come off second best. But just as hang-gliders need a steep ridge and a steady wind in order to soar, so do model pterodactyls, and I too had been waiting impatiently all weekend for the wind. It was unfortunate from my point of view that a hang-glider had chosen the same ridge as myself, for a photograph of the monster keeping company with a hang-glider would have destroyed any semblance of palaeontological accuracy, and would have greatly lessened its appeal to the producer of the programme. I therefore allowed it to stray far along the ridge to the left, hoping that our group, including the photographer, would follow. But I failed to reckon with the increasing turbulence of the wind, and the powerful eddy at the far end of the slope. *Pteranodon* started to lose height in a sideslip, and became reluctant to turn back into the wind. Finally I resorted to diving him back towards us, but by this time he was losing height fast and was well below the lift area. On top of this, it had started to rain. As a sheet of heavy drops swept over us, obscuring the model from view, I heard a splintering crash from the foot of the slope, and knew the worst had happened.

Impatient to see the extent of the damage, I scrambled down the steep grassy hillside, which had become wet and treacherous. The slight depression down which I was making my way had turned into a miniature waterfall – a natural waterslide with a mud bottom, 150 feet high. I skidded down this unexpected short cut on my behind, losing my transmitter

and tools as I fell, until my progress was arrested by a crunching sound: I had fallen exactly on top of the already damaged remains of *Pteranodon*.

We picked up the pieces and carried them to the car. The car, of course, turned out to have a puncture.

The Curse of the Black Mountains had not finished with us yet. Soaked, muddy and despondent, we finally returned with the remains of *Pteranodon* to our host, the bookseller Richard Booth in Hay-on-Wye, for hot baths and elderberry wine. There was, I remember, a home-grown goose on the dinner menu, which had a remarkably consoling effect, and our spirits started to rise. After dinner Mike Marten set out on the long drive back to London. Halfway along the M40, he had another puncture (the first one had not been mended yet since it was Sunday evening). The motorway telephone was out of order. Eventually a passing motorist was flagged down, and after a very long wait an AA patrolman arrived. He had no means of mending the puncture, but alerted an all-night garage in Uxbridge, which sent a breakdown vehicle. After another long wait the breakdown vehicle arrived and the car was taken in tow, but after two miles the 'breakdown' vehicle did exactly that. Its throttle cable had snapped. At 8.30 the next morning a caravanserai of two broken-down vehicles containing a group of thoroughly broken-spirited people, was towed by a large truck into a garage on the outskirts of Uxbridge.

FOG-BOUND BOOTH

Rugby (Union) football is of all sports the most prone to fog. The fogs of the Thirties were much worse than any England gets today, and December 1934 was a vintage fog month. At the start of the Otley vs. Headingley match, four days before Christmas, visibility was poor on the Otley pitch. All that spectators could make out was a vague blur of figures moving about in the penumbra beyond the drooping near-side corner flags.

Occasionally the ball would soar up above the murk, but otherwise there was no indication of the state of play, although muffled sporadic cries such as 'Feet, feet, use your feet!' could sometimes be heard.

L. A. Booth, that great wing three-quarter, was playing centre for once. It has been said that the distinctive quality of Booth's play – which so often won the day for Headingley, for Yorkshire, and for England – consisted of remaining inconspicuous for long periods of time, so that the opposing side would be caught off-guard by his sudden bursts of swerving footwork and prodigious long passes. But his low-profile tactics were of little use on this occasion, since none of the other players could be seen either – and what was the use of a long pass when it could not be properly aimed?

Booth scored Headingley's first try, but failed to score again.

At half time Headingley were leading 6–3, but as the gloom intensified the scales tipped in favour of Otley. (After all, they were on home ground. Perhaps they could feel where they were with their feet.) The play grew more and more confused and cries of 'penalty' and waves of cheering became more frequent as it became harder and harder for anyone to know whether he was off-side. The game ended in a disastrous 11–6 defeat for Headingley.

A roll-call was held in the dressing-rooms after the match and two players were discovered to be missing. They were found still standing on the field, forlornly hoping that the ball might eventually come their way.

9

Politics, Aggression and War

'Sport is no solution to political tension.'
– George Orwell

I SEE U-2

During a briefing in Chicago on 16th September 1970 Henry Kissinger uttered a stern though veiled threat to the Soviet Union: any attempt to base Soviet nuclear-armed submarines in Cuba would have the gravest consequences. American intelligence reports on Cuba had recently given rise to alarming suspicions, but as yet there was no proof. Kissinger would be keeping an eye on the Russians.

On that very day a U-2 spy plane flying in the thin upper atmosphere above the Caribbean country was taking a series of photographs that Kissinger would have to act upon. The photographs showed a harbour at Cienfuegos on the south coast, a picturesque inlet and a bay dotted with small islands. One of the islands, Cayo Alcatraz, had already attracted attention when U-2 photographs taken a few weeks earlier showed a new barracks under construction. Now there was incontrovertible evidence that a submarine base was being prepared: the spy plane photographed submarine tenders in the bay moored to permanent buoys. There was a new dock, fuel storage facilities, and a major array of communications equipment, with radar and anti-aircraft missiles to defend the entire complex.

Was this merely an upgrading of Cuba's own defences, or a more aggressively menacing, Russian-manned base of a permanent nature? The adroit diplomat called upon his vast experience of foreign affairs and concluded that one piece of evidence in the reconnaissance photographs stamped the whole project as indelibly Russian: the soccer and basketball fields which had just been laid out. Kissinger, an old soccer fan, recalled that the the Cubans do not play soccer.

A series of diplomatic exchanges of the most vital and intricate nature took place. Once again, as in the missile crisis of 1962, one false move might have plunged the world into nuclear war. But the astute Kissinger, acting on his sporting instincts, saved us from Armageddon.

He was right, but for the wrong reason. Cubans are, in fact, very keen on soccer, and have been ever since Fidel Castro took power. The soccer fields on Cayo Alcatraz continued to be used by the islanders long after the Russians departed. And at their next encounter the Cubans rubbed the point home to their Yankee neighbours by defeating the American side 5-nil.

But the military, it seems, will never learn. During a CIA press conference in Washington in March 1982 aerial photographs were shown to reporters as evidence of Soviet interference in Nicaraguan affairs. After being shown pictures of Soviet-built ETR-64 armoured personnel carriers the group were told: 'There's the Soviet physical training area equipped with chin bars and other types of equipment to exercise the forces, and a running track.' As *Spectator* reporter Nicholas von Hoffman commented: 'Next the Russians will have parallel bars and gymnastic rings throughout the entire isthmus. Will it end anywhere short of the Olympics?'

BANG ON COURSE

At the twelfth tee of the Elephant Hills Course near Victoria Falls a regular hazard used to be the crocodiles – indeed the course boasts its own 'special rule', like others noted elsewhere in these pages, which reads: 'If a ball is eaten another may be dropped in its place.' The course is thick with giant baobab trees, while warthog, waterbuck and baboons regularly trot down the fairways. In the damper sections of the course there are hippopotami; in the rough elephants roam.

During the November 1976 Classic Golf Tournament at this course there was a little local difficulty – a terrorist attack. And so it was that another 'special rule' was added to the others: 'A stroke is to be played again if interrupted by gunfire or a sudden explosion.'

THE FUTBOL WAR

George Orwell's remarks about the danger of sport increasing national rivalries, in his 1946 essay 'The Sporting Spirit', were to prove strangely prophetic. He was commenting on the 'goodwill tour' of the Moscow Dynamos in the winter of 1945 which, as he pointed out, was a fiasco from every angle. The fog-bound 3–3 draw against Chelsea at Stamford Bridge was hardly a great propaganda victory. But things went from bad to worse, and at the Arsenal a British and a Russian player came to blows and the crowd booed the referee. The Glasgow match was a free-for-all. This reminded Orwell of scenes he had witnessed in Burma, where the supporters of one side would break through the police and disable their opponents' goalkeeper. For, as he points out, in young countries where games-playing and nationalism are both recent developments, even fiercer passions are aroused.

In one instance at least, the mixture of sport and national rivalry has led not just to street violence and unruly scenes among the crowds, but to outright hostilities between two countries, with real aeroplanes bombing – and killing – helpless citizens in the approved fashion.

El Salvador and Honduras, with their common border and their history of tense national rivalry, have long been the tinderbox of Central America. A 1958 treaty intended to resolve the tensions had not helped: its main result was that hordes of settlers crossed from over-populated El Salvador to Honduras in search of work and land. This created fresh resentments, and skirmishes again broke out in 1967. Following a tour by Lyndon Johnson a temporary improvement in relations was achieved; then in 1969 by an extraordinarily unlucky coincidence the two countries found that their soccer teams had been drawn to face each other in the final round of World Cup qualifying competitions for the Central and North American region.

In the first match on 8th June Honduras won, on home

ground. This resulted in fierce riots. A week later there was another match, this time in El Salvador. El Salvador won. More and fiercer riots ensued and by 24th June El Salvador found it necessary to declare a state of siege. The third and decisive match, played in Mexico, resulted in victory for El Salvador. Stung by this defeat, Honduras retaliated by accusing El Salvador of 'an invasion of agricultural settlers'. Both parties then appealed to the Interamerican Commission on Human Rights, but a few days later there were mutual accusations of violations of air space and attacks on border troops. On 14th July El Salvador invaded Honduras. Honduras replied with bombs and 3,000 people died in the first four days of fighting. The conflict, which became known as the 'Futbol War', has rumbled on for many years, with occasional truces. For example, both El Salvador and Honduras qualified for the 1982 World Cup Finals, taking first and second places in the CONCACAF playoff qualification tournament held in Honduras. No shots were fired on that occasion but there seems no sign of any satisfactory permanent resolution of the problem to the present day.

ITALIAN ROAD HAZARDS

In the summer of 1946 one of the most disastrous cycle races of all time took place when an Italian team from Venezia Giulia crossed the border near a town called Pieris. The race, the final stage of the Tour of Italy, was scheduled to end at Trieste, perhaps not the happiest of choices in view of the tense atmosphere between Italy and Yugoslavia. As the cyclists crossed the border of Venezia Giulia they saw that the road was heavily strewn with nails, barbed wire and bricks. They were threading their way through these obstacles when a hail of stones from Slovenes hidden behind the bushes brought them to a halt. Cycles were smashed and shots were fired at the police escort, which returned the fire. One of the team was killed, and 30 were injured. Tens of thousands of Italians were in Trieste to welcome the cyclists, and when the news of the action at Pieris reached them a riot ensued: the headquarters of the Communist Party were sacked and furniture was burned in the streets. The Slovenes counter-demonstrated and general strikes were declared in both countries which lasted for several days.

These post-war years were difficult times for cyclists in Italy. A vast number of people were going about on bicycles, for since petrol was so scarce it had become the principal means of individual transport. In the general confusion which abounded many people went missing, including the daughter of an important functionary of the American Embassy in Rome. She had last been seen by friends, making her way back to Rome on her bicycle from near Rieti – a town some 50 miles north of the capital, near the foothills of the Abruzzi mountains. When the girl failed to appear after a day, searches were made along the route, and a strange and most gruesome sporting hazard was revealed.

Nerola is a pretty hillside village – a cluster of houses round a bend in the road. At this very bend there were two shops next to each other, one a cycle repair shop and the other a butcher's, whose sausages, in this time of meat shortage, were considered the best for miles around. The shops were owned by the same man, who became known as the Monster of Nerola after it was discovered that he was in the habit of scattering tacks on the road near the bend. This ensured a good supply of customers for the cycle shop of this Italian Sweeney Todd. Many of them were never seen again.

TANAKA'S SANDWICH

In the autumn of 1973, when a Japanese diplomatic mission including Prime Minister Kakuei Tanaka and the Foreign Minister was visiting Britain, somebody suggested that it would make a nice day out for them all to go down to Sandwich and have a few rounds of golf. The Japanese are extremely keen golfers – there are golf courses all over the Japanese archipelago, and yet they still often find themselves queueing to tee off.

The only British Cabinet Minister at the time with a reasonably low handicap was Mr Whitelaw. A lot of thought was given to arranging the golf match and it was decided, in order to avoid possible diplomatic embarrassment, to make up a foursome: Tanaka was partnered by Alec Hill of the Royal St George's Club, and Whitelaw played alongside the Japanese Foreign Minister.

On the day selected Sandwich was enjoying one of its famous Force 8 gales. The distinguished party struggled round the course, balls flying all over the place, trying desperately to imagine that they were having a good time. With statesmanlike tact Whitelaw allowed his side to lose to Tanaka's by four and three.

WAR STOPPED PLAY

In his war memoirs Lord Alanbrooke describes General Eisenhower on the links at Rheims shortly before the Battle of the Bulge, putting away, 'entirely detached and taking no part in running the war'. The White House was stung to reply. In November 1959 the Press Secretary, James Hagerty, issued a statement: the President never held a club in his hand from the moment of the Allied landing until the war was over in Europe in May 1945. Hagerty did, however, concede that the President had hit a few balls while in England, before the D-Day invasion.

During a television interview in 1961 Eisenhower shed further light on his attitude to the relative importance of golf and world affairs. While playing golf in 1955 he was called back to the clubhouse from the fourth hole by a telephone call from the State Department. 'It was some little emergency,' he said, not immediately urgent. Just as he was getting back to his game he was again summoned. It was another call about the same problem, and again he told them it could wait until he finished his game. Finally, there was a third call, from someone who didn't know about the other two calls. By this time the President's temper was completely out of control: so much so that not long afterwards he suffered a heart attack, which he attributed directly to people interrupting his game.

TROUBLE ON T'MOORS

When one of the Earl of Derby's footmen went berserk and shot both the butler and the under-butler at Knowsley Park in 1952 a wag at White's Club commented afterwards: 'Can't blame the fellow, really – not often you get a left and a right in butlers.'

Tragic accidents on the moors were few. Beaters, it is true, took a certain risk. They were generally recruited, willy-nilly, from the ranks of the poor and oppressed – farm labourers working on the estates of the Lord and Master, and other lackeys of the ruling, and shooting, classes. Herded to the scene of action in carts, fed out of sacks, and dressed in makeshift uniforms to facilitate manoeuvres and exclude disruptive elements, their role in serving the sporting interests of their masters has never been enviable. From time to time cries would reach the ears of 'the quality' as they wielded their Purdeys, and from the motley figures scurrying about in the brushwood there would be admiring comments: 'Master do be a wonderful fine shot – clean took hat off me head and never touched I', or more feelingly, 'Ouch, Master have got I again!'

At one shoot the head beater hit upon the bright idea of improving organization and morale by painting a single letter on each beater's smock, so that they could be arranged in neat alphabetical order: A upwind of B; B to the northeast of C; and so on. For some unaccountable reason the beaters did not take kindly to this degree of regimentation, and while Lords and Ladies were having lunch four of the more unruly letters arranged themselves into a short Anglo-Saxon word which left their Ladyships in no doubt about the strength of their feelings.

The older beaters developed a certain cunning and know-how under fire. A beater at Six Mile Bottom, when King Edward VII was shooting with Sir Ernest Cassel, managed to get shot in the knee by His Majesty. The King had been enjoying a lively conversation with a young lady when she suddenly pointed at a hare which had started up. Not realizing that there was a beater in the bushes some distance behind the hare, the King took aim at the animal and fired. The beater's sudden yell of agony failed to impinge upon the royal ear, for wild cries and scuffles in spinneys are all part of the background of a shoot. The man was not too badly wounded to hobble out from his hiding place in the spinney, unnoticed by His Majesty, who was still talking to the young lady at his side. Sir George Holford, a royal equerry, realizing what had happened, approached the King and told him he had shot a beater.

The beater, visions of royal rewards and life pensions floating before his eyes, made a great show of his injury, hopping around and moaning dramatically. The King naturally became

extremely upset and saw to it that the old fellow, who clearly 'knew exactly the value of being in the right place at the right time', spent the rest of his life enjoying the just rewards of having served His Majesty under fire.

THE ATTACKING BUGATTI

In 1949 a visiting French cycling team entered for the Tour of Italy was pelted with stones and rotten eggs by the Italian fans. The Italian *campionissimo*, Fausto Coppi, would probably have won even more easily than he did without this sort of aggressive behaviour on his behalf, but it is just one more unpleasant example of how national rivalry can take on war-like overtones during a sporting event.

The following year the Italian cyclist Gino Bartali took part in the Tour de France race, and fared even less well. A taciturn and deeply religious man, Bartali had retired to a monastery during the Second World War, and was the very opposite of a belligerent, nationalistic sportsman. Yet his presence in the event was bitterly resented by the French fans, one of whom went to extraordinary lengths to express his feelings.

The Pyrénéean section is one of the most testing portions of the French cycle race. As Bartali reached the crest of the Mont Aspin pass, pushing ahead to consolidate his lead, he was struck in the goggles by a well-aimed pebble. The goggles were smashed but Bartali cycled on, plunging furiously down the steep hairpin bends on the other side, to be met by a jeering crowd of Frenchmen. Pushing through the abusive throng he sped on down the valley. Then, in the distance, he heard the crackling whine of the exhaust of a racing Bugatti. The sound grew closer. Rushing through the winding French roads and over stone bridges, poplars and roadside hoardings flashing by, Bartali heard the exhaust note change in pitch as the Bugatti sighted its prey and moved in for the kill – for Bartali would indeed have been killed had he not leaped from his bicycle onto a grassy bank at the last instant, as the maniac motorist roared past at 60 mph, silk scarf streaming in the wind, the number plate obscured in the swirling dust.

The driver was never traced.

At the next checkpoint the local population went for the Italians with sticks, though the great French cyclist Louison Bobet indignantly tried to beat them off. In the end the police had to rescue the Italians, who refused, not surprisingly, to have anything more to do with the race.

CASTE AND CLASS

Not only the struggle between nations, but the struggle between the classes can intervene in sport with grotesque results. An example of this was the unfortunate table tennis player from mainland China, Lee Fu Young. The single fault of this otherwise brilliant player was that, in terms of the politics of China in the mid 1960s, he came from too high a class. Although Lee Fu Young had embraced the principles of Mao's glorious revolution with as much enthusiasm as any sportsman can be expected to display towards politics, his family were of Mandarin extraction: it would not have done for him to win too often or too decisively. In three successive finals of the National Table Tennis Championships he allowed himself to be beaten by Chuang Tse Chuang.

There is no question in the minds of observers of these

championships that this is what was happening, for Lee Fu Young was clearly the better player. The only parallel in western sport would be the professional tennis player who, anxious to get in as many tournaments as possible to increase his fees, allows himself to be beaten in the opening round so that he can go on to the next event and collect his appearance money. One day two such deliberate losers will meet in a tournament, and an interesting fiasco should result.

The current Chinese table tennis 'fall guy' is Lee Shen Shi. He is not allowed to win two matches consecutively, and his role appears to be to bolster the morale of fellow players of humbler but ideologically more acceptable origins.

The closest analogy in western politics to this curious state of affairs was perhaps the case of King Constantine of Greece, who gained his Olympic gold medal in yachting in the Dragon class at Naples in 1960. (The Russians, in the same year, won the Star class – using an American boat with American sails!) In 1968, as Vice President of the International Yacht Race Union, King Constantine made a final effort to organize a Greek entry into the America's Cup event for 1970, which was to be held at Newport, Rhode Island. Money was no problem: the Greek shipping millionaires were all on the King's side, and his superb expertise as helmsman might well have given the Greek entry a leading position. The only difficulty was that, being King, Constantine found it impossible to obtain the stamp of official approval from the prevailing regime in his country; for the Colonels were in power, and the last thing they wanted was to give any semblance of support to the man they had deposed.

BANDITS' BEND

Pat Carlsson (Pat Moss) and Geraint (Gerry) Phillips were driving an Austin 1300 GT provided by the Jamaican importer during the Carreras 1000 Jamaican Rally in September 1971. The car was taking considerable punishment on roads which varied from the soft mud of sugar cane plantations to narrow stony tracks on which punctures were a regular occurrence. Among the problems they encountered in the first twenty-four hours were clutch failure (the pedal pin fell out) and a quick-lift jack which didn't – making changing tyres a laborious business.

There was a compulsory seven-hour break on the second day, Saturday, and Stirling Moss was able to help them with servicing arrangements. Refreshed after their brief sleep the two drivers set off at 6.30 that evening for the second stage of the rally. Inevitably they were well behind cars like the Triumph 2.5 PI, the BMW 2002 and the Volvo 144S which were among the competitors, but the scenery was magnificent, there was a spectacular sunset, and their spirits were high as they raced through the gathering dusk.

Shortly after nightfall they noticed some headlights gradually getting larger behind them on a road section. Thinking it was another competitor Pat allowed the car to pass, but it turned out to be a rather battered Morris Oxford Estate which they had not noticed among the entries for the rally. In it were five unkempt but determined-looking Jamaicans.

Red tail-lights disappeared into the distance, but after a little while they noticed the red lights growing rapidly larger. Suddenly the Morris Oxford swerved violently across their front, ramming the 1300 and forcing it into the bank. Four extremely tough Jamaicans got out. One of them was reaching into the left side of his jacket with his right hand, and all of them had very unfriendly expressions.

Deciding that this was no place for a chat, Pat reversed out, pulled up on the bank on the other side of the Oxford, and drove off. As she pulled away the would-be bandits leapt back into their car and rammed her on the other side. But she had picked up speed and was driving as fast as the 1300 would go down the narrow road. The Oxford screeched off in furious pursuit. Gradually they gained on the Austin 1300, taking desperate chances with the winding treacherous road. No matter what Pat did she could not shake them off and she couldn't go any faster for fear of skidding over the cliff into the sea. The Morris Oxford tried time and time again to force them off the road, swerving violently behind them, inches away from their rear bumper. (The thought struck them that if the driver of that Morris Oxford ever gave up banditry and took up rally driving he would make a formidable opponent.)

After a dozen miles of this Pat saw a sharp, dangerous-looking right-hand bend ahead. They were travelling very fast – too fast – as they came into the bend, and they mounted the left bank, screaming round on a wall of death. As they came out again onto the straight they looked into the rear-view mirror and saw a blur of red and white lights as the Oxford spun and rolled over into the bank.

After this, the remainder of the rally seemed plain sailing: the battery split, roads flooded, a funeral brought all traffic to a standstill and they got lost in a cane plantation. But it was with a feeling of some relief and achievement that the two drivers finally arrived at the National Stadium in Kingston on Sunday night.

Alas, they were not on the winning list. They were disqualified for forcing a non-competing car off the road.

10
Pigs, Libbers and Switch-Hitters

'I know I have the body of a weak and feeble woman, but I have the heart and stomach of a king.'

– Queen Elizabeth I

My first real contact with women in sport came when I learned to repeat Thomas Inch's weightlifting stunt, balancing two girls on the 'scales of justice', and raising the whole contraption into the air with my right arm. This took much practice and taught me a lot about the female temperament. Of course many women in sport have been found to have not only the heart and stomach of a king, but other male attributes as well. There have also been defectors on both sides of the sex war. What a waste.

THE ROYALL TREATMENT

While he was President of the United States, John Quincy Adams (1825–29) used to rise before dawn and dash down to the Potomac River for an early morning swim. On most days he would be out, dried and dressed before the sun was up, full of energy for the Presidential labours which awaited him. Twice, however, things went not quite to plan.

On one occasion the President decided to paddle across the river in a canoe and swim back, but the canoe filled with water in midstream and sank. Trying to swim in his sodden clothing was too much of a struggle, so Adams stripped them off as he swam and arrived back at the White House only half dressed.

Normally clothes were no problem – he simply took them off, left them on the bank and swam as nature intended. The formidable female reporter Anne Royall took advantage of this carefree habit of the President's on another occasion, when trying to get an interview on a subject 'of vital importance to the nation' (the State Bank question). She immobilized him by sitting on his clothes.

Adams suggested that she should retire behind a bush while he 'made his toilet', promising to give her an interview as soon as he was fully dressed. But Anne Royall was not going to be cajoled into losing her advantage. She pointed out that there were three fishermen just around the next bend, and she would start screaming if he made so much as a move towards the clothes, on which she remained firmly seated. Sensing defeat, President Adams gave the interview – up to his chin in the Potomac.

CHARGETTES FIRED

American football teams have long been proud of their female cheerleaders, who put on baton-twirling displays before major events to raise the morale of the team. Their names associate them with the team they represent – for instance the Dallas Cowboys have the Dallas Cowgirls, while the Los Angeles Rams rejoice in their Embraceable Ewes. The San Diego Chargers have a group known as the Chargettes – or rather they did until October 1978 when the whole bevy were fired because one of their number was identified in a *Playboy* magazine centrespread.

The story of the Chargettes was relayed in the local press by a woman reporter whose anger went beyond sisterly sympathy. The concept of female cheerleaders was, it seems, one of the ugliest symptoms of the piggishness of the typical male chauvinist, and the idea of one of these monsters having the hypocritical gall to fire a girl just because she had accepted a job with *Playboy*, that other bastion of male chauvinism, was the last straw.

Thus when women established – thanks to a legal action – the important privilege of being allowed, like male sports reporters, to enter players' locker rooms, baseball sportsmen everywhere trembled and invested in protective clothing. But the women failed to take advantage of their victory. For a start, they agreed to talk to players for fifteen minutes only, during which time the players were to remain fully clothed. Worse still, many of the women at first could not think of any relevant queries. As Reggie Jackson of the Yankees remarked: 'I don't object, but they don't ask serious questions.'

The most common question asked by women reporters was: 'How do you feel about women reporters being allowed into your locker room?'

MORNING CLOUD UNRUFFLED

John Belcher, the well-known yachtsman and director of Baron Instruments Ltd, developed a highly successful technique for distracting the opposition while rounding a buoy in a race. Noticeable among his crew were a number of elegant and seductive young ladies, one of whom would stand beside him on the foredeck, entwining herself round him as he manhandled the sails during critical phases of a race. The crew of nearby yachts rounding a marker would become so fascinated by the spectacle that they would devote more attention to the girl than to their own spinnakers, which would invariably end up entwined round the forestay. Meanwhile Belcher's spinnaker, with its characteristic mailed fist symbol, would be smartly stowed and he would be beating along the next tack, ahead of the fleet.

The only time Belcher's stratagem completely failed was in the Solent during a Point Championships race, when the boat he was trying to distract was *Morning Cloud* – Mark I, the 34-foot version. Edward Heath and his staunch crew were above being diverted by this sort of thing, and Belcher became more distracted than they were. A chalice was duly raised to Heath during the celebration dinner, and the toast was: 'To a man of iron will and purpose.'

A PIG IS THRASHED

The sex war on the tennis courts reached its peak in 1973. In April of that year the 1939 Wimbledon Champion, Bobby Riggs, opened the offensive by challenging the 30-year-old women's champion Margaret Court to a £4,150 winner-take-all match at Ramona, California. In a sneak attack the male element inflicted damage on Mrs Court's morale right from the start: her 14-month-old son Danny threw her only pair of tennis shoes into the hotel bedroom lavatory. It was Mother's Day, so possibly some form of comment was implied by the infant. Luckily the shoes dried out just in time for the match.

Riggs, then fifty-five, kept Mrs Court guessing by varying his game so that she was unable to develop her own rhythm. She appeared tense and nervous, and showed none of the aggression she would have needed to penetrate her opponent's admittedly lightweight defences. In such cases it is essential to carry the action firmly into enemy territory. The morale-boosting effect of uniform cannot be overstressed. Mrs Court unwisely selected a fetching lime-green and gold outfit for the match. She should have worn icy white or dominating black.

The decisive battle of the sex war occurred in September of the same year, when Billie Jean King challenged Bobby Riggs at the Houston Astrodome – a colossally impressive stadium, with more than its fair share of loudspeakers and floodlights. Riggs was delighted at the challenge, saying, 'I want her – she's the women's libber leader.'

Mrs King fully understood the importance of impressing her enemy. She arrived in the Astrodome on a gold triumphal litter, borne by male athletes from a neighbouring university. Alighting, she presented Riggs with a small live pig. Riggs arrived dressed as Henry VIII in a rickshaw drawn by six professional models. On his lap was a photograph of a naked woman, in one hand a bone on which he gnawed. In return for the pig he presented Billie Jean King with a 6-foot-long lollipop, remarking: 'You're going to be a sucker for my lobs.'

All this was watched by the 30,000 spectators in the Astrodome, not to mention the 48-million audience of the ABC television network. For the first time the sex war was being enacted before a mass audience, with all the showmanship American television could muster, and the tennis match itself was subsidiary to the dramatization of sexual hostilities. The game was not glorious. Rex Bellamy of *The Times* remarked that 'the average first round loser in an average men's singles at Wimbledon could have beaten the pair of them in successive matches.' Riggs was tired, and seemed shaky on his pins, and although he managed to break Mrs King's serve, she had no difficulty in giving him all and more than he was able to hand out. He was beaten 6–4, 6–3, 6–3, and Mrs King went away with the $100,000 prize money.

Riggs was not daunted: 'I'll put Billie Jean and all the other women's libbers back where they belong – in the kitchen and the bedroom.'

Mrs King's reply was characteristically cool: 'Give me 24 hours and a beer and I'll think about it.'

DOUBLE AGENTS

A Swiss skier, Hedy Schlunegger, who won an Olympic gold medal for the women's downhill in 1948 (her time was 2 minutes 28.3 seconds), surprised everyone by returning the following year, after a visit to Heidelberg University hospital, to compete in the men's events. While his performance in this was creditable, he found it harder to defeat the opposition, and did not come among the winners.

Defectors – or double agents – in the opposite direction have been more numerous. One of the earliest was the racing driver Robert Cowell, who became Roberta Cowell, without any noticeable improvement in driving skill.

In August 1977 it was revealed that a male tennis player, Richard Raskind, had defected, going over to the other side to become Renee Richards. She was debarred from taking part in women's events by the organizers of the US Open Tennis Championships, but in a surprising court case a New York judge ruled that it was 'grossly unfair, discriminative and inequitable' of the organizers of the Open to institute the sex-test in order to prevent Richards playing in the competition.

GRACE'S PLEASURE

Many have suspected that W. G. Grace was something of a male chauvinist pig. Certainly cricket mattered more to him than the pleasures of female company, though an incident which occurred in 1872 suggests that the two concepts may have been more deeply connected in his subconscious than is generally realized.

While batting at Glasgow he hit a ball out of the field and into the lap of a 'sweet, unoffending' lady in a passing cab. The bowler Alf Shaw, *à propos* of this incident remarked, with a deep insight into the workings of Grace's mind: 'It's like this: I puts the ball where I pleases and Mr Grace puts it where he pleases.'

UNILATERAL DECLARATION OF PEACE

Mrs George Chuvalo finally won the battle against sport by taking unilateral action. In August 1970 she leapt into the ring twice to stop the fight between her husband George, the Canadian heavyweight boxer, and the American George Foreman, who was giving him a ferocious pounding.

'His eyes were getting bloodshot,' Mrs Chuvalo explained. 'He had that glazed look, and he was spitting blood.'

By the third round she really felt she had had enough and, thanks to her insistence, the fight was in fact ended. She had already intervened in an earlier contest against Joe Frazier, and in her view it was time for George to give up boxing for good.

'He won't use his head,' she declared. 'I've tried again and again to get him to quit.'

At last she was successful. Wives of soccer fans and Sunday golfing widows everywhere should make her their patron saint.

11
Odd Numbers

'There is divinity in odd numbers'
– The Merry Wives of Windsor, V.i.2.

THAT SINKING FEELING

The Oxford and Cambridge Boat Race has resulted in five sinkings: Cambridge in 1857, both crews in 1912, Oxford in 1925 and 1951, and Cambridge again in 1978. The honours are thus equally shared. (During the last sinking a French television commentator was heard to remark: 'Now the Cambridge crew are going to drink an early cup of tea.')

As to the cause of these fiascos, though weather was undoubtedly a contributory factor, as well as the low freeboard of some of the eights, the 'Red' Dean of Canterbury, Dr Hewlett Johnson, speaking in April 1951, advanced an altogether novel theory. Shortly after the Oxford sinking of that year the Dean's words were read out over Moscow Radio, on the occasion of the Soviet authorities presenting him with the Stalin Peace Prize. He mentioned the Boat Race sinking, and stated that he was ashamed that the cox of the Oxford crew was an American student. It was the presence of this American in the Oxford boat which caused Oxford to lose the race. An identical fate, he proclaimed, awaited the Royal Navy, which was under American command.

Similar divine interventions in meteorology may have been responsible for a curious double fiasco which occurred on 6th August 1945. Lightning struck the press box at Lord's cricket ground, putting the phone out of action and bringing down part of the ceiling. Another flash incapacitated the loudspeaker system at the White City. (6th August 1945 was the day the Americans dropped the first atomic bomb on Hiroshima.)

THE MATHEMATICS OF COINCIDENCE

Few writers will admit how many of life's major events are ruled by coincidence. They bring coincidence nervously and clumsily into their plots, as though it were something to be ashamed of. But almost everything that happens is caused by the chance interaction of trains of events which have been set in motion long before.

Although sport generally tries to eliminate chance happenings wherever possible, coincidence does intervene, and a fiasco usually results. The long distance walker Norman Read, who won an Olympic gold medal in the 50 kilometres event in Melbourne in 1956, was involved in a particularly fascinating chance incident in which the slow machinations of fate, the inexorable progress towards what must have been one of the most infuriating moments in any sportsman's life, can be plotted with some accuracy.

It would be necessary, for a full understanding of what happened, to know why the walking race in which Norman Read took part that afternoon in 1959 started at exactly 5.09 pm. Some fateful event delayed what was intended to be a 5.00 race by just nine minutes. Did half the walkers arrive at Palmerston South instead of Palmerston North? Was there fluff in the public address system, or mud in the starter's pistol? We shall never know. The route of the race was circuitous, beginning and ending not far from the centre of Palmerston North. It was a stage in the 1959 New Zealand Championships—the 20 kilometres 'heel and toe'.

Things in those days were measured in miles and feet, so as far as Palmerston North was concerned it was not a 20 kilometres race but a 12.427 mile race. Keeping to miles, it should be noted that the town of Fielding lies exactly 12 miles to the south of

Palmerston. At precisely 45 seconds after 5.38 pm a freight train 704 feet long left Fielding on a slow and laborious journey towards Palmerston North, clocking up an average speed of 16 mph and making on the way two stops: a quickie of 7½ seconds and a more leisurely pause of 12 minutes 30 seconds.

Thus, as Norman Read was striding round the 12.427 mile course at an average pace of 7.9985 miles an hour, the freight train was approaching Palmerston North at almost, but not quite, twice the speed that he was.

At this point it must be explained that just one mile south of the town of Palmerston North there is a level crossing, and that the route of the walking race took the walkers over this crossing at .296 miles from the finishing line of the race. To save the reader from further suspense—yes, the train *did* arrive at the crossing at precisely 6.40 pm, and this was indeed exactly one half-second ahead of Norman Read: one half-second being the time it took the cowcatcher on the front of the train to cross the central point of the level crossing. But behind the cowcatcher was the engine, and behind the engine was the tender, and behind the tender there were 1,289 wagons, freight cars and low-loaders—or so it seemed to the walker, as he danced up and down in a fury of expectation, doing mental arithmetic to pass the time, while the 704 feet of freight train crawled by at 23.46 feet per second, taking just 30.0085 seconds to do so, and as the figure of his main rival in the race, Kevin Keogh of Australia, who had arrived at the crossing at 6.39 and 58 seconds, rapidly became a speck in the distance.

LUCKY ESCAPES

People who do dangerous things with cars in the name of sport come to expect extraordinary happenings as everyday events. Some kind of divine intervention seems to bail them out from lethal situations at the last minute.

In the early days of stock-car racing in the United States the 'good 'ole boys' used to get into some crazy situations. Charlotte, North Carolina was one of the first places to boast regular stock-car events, and in 1955 a stock-car racer – a heavy-drinking, hard man given to chewing on the butts of old cigars and doing unkind things to motor cars – had a disagreement with the law concerning moonshine liquor.

One evening the law caught up with this individual at his motel, and a chase ensued. The police followed him, elbows out and eyeballs contra-rotating, and eventually the 'good 'ole boy's' car ran wide on a corner, smashed through a fence, reared up and went end-over-end through a chicken run, tore across the yard of the chicken farm, through a barn and into a pond, where the driver was found hanging by his straps upside down in a very battered vehicle, trying to light a cigar with a wet match.

The Sheriff peered at him through the smashed windscreen.

'Boy, you sure are lucky to be alive – I sure as hell thought you'd killed yourself,' said the Sheriff.

'Killed myself!' the unruffled Tar Heel scoffed. 'What the hell d'you think I am – a stunt man?'

In the South African Kyalami nine-hours race the Australian driver Frank Gardner, sharing an AC Cobra with Bob Althoff of South Africa, showed that a crash is not the end of a race for a resourceful driver.

They had been racing for many hours, and night had fallen. As he was rounding a corner Althoff left the road, jumped the ditch, and bent the Cobra. Disconsolately, he walked back to the pits and announced: 'I'm sorry, Frank, I've crashed the car.'

Frank went down to have a look. The car was standing on its wheels, but it was on the wrong side of the ditch, a few yards from the bank which bordered the track at this point. Not being one to accept defeat readily, Frank did some quick thinking. Pacing out the distance between the bank and the ditch he calculated that if Althoff could get up enough speed he should be able to jump the ditch and re-enter the race. The chief danger lay in the oncoming cars, whose headlights swept by at regular intervals as they roared through the darkness. If the leap worked, the car would be rejoining the track at right angles to the traffic. He looked at the car again. One headlight was pointing at the sky, the other somewhat sideways, and there was a dent in the front. Otherwise it did not look too bad.

'I think you can do it, Bob,' said Frank. He watched the headlights sweep round the corner, as one car after another screamed past them through the night. At last there was a gap. 'Now!'

Althoff slammed the racing engine into first gear, and with gravel and mud flying in all directions accelerated towards the ditch, leapt over, spun round in the middle of the track, and roared off into the darkness—to place second in the race.

Learning from this incident, Frank Gardner became famous for his refusal to give up after a crash. While racing at Le Mans, sharing a big works Ford with an Indianapolis track driver named Roger McCluskey, Gardner had the same experience of seeing his co-driver approach the pits, helmet in hand, to announce defeat.

'Well, I'm afraid that's it Frank, we've had a little accident.'

Refusing to accept that this could mean the end of the race, Gardner asked how badly the car was damaged.

'It's a little bit bent,' was all McCluskey would say.

The two men walked back along the top of the perimeter bank, under the floodlights, with the cars rushing past them, and eventually came upon a piece of metal. Frank looked at it. It was the radiator from his car. Another few yards further on they came upon a wheel. Frank recognized it as his. Then, walking on another 20 yards they encountered a twisted metal object, rather like a piece of modern sculpture. It was the front half of the chassis. Gardner confronted his partner. 'Where's the rest of it?'

The remaining evidence of McCluskey's 'little accident' was

scattered in small pieces for 200 yards along the bank of the Le Mans circuit.

Ivor Bueb, driving a Lister Jaguar at Oulton Park in 1968, leapt off the track and landed in the lake. When the wreckage was examined, it was found to be transfixed by a metal stake. Luckily it had missed Bueb. Immediately next to the car was another hefty metallic object which turned out to be an unexploded land mine.

Death is never far away from the cockpit of a racing car, although today only a tiny fraction of the spectacular crashes the public so often enjoy watching actually result in fatalities. Improvements in design and safety measures have made motor racing a very much safer sport. In earlier years things were more nerve-racking.

When the Ford GT was first introduced the driver Bruce McLaren, using one of these cars at Le Mans, started experiencing a high-speed misfire. This is a difficult fault to detect in the workshop, and the engineers had failed to trace the origin of the problem. So McLaren took one of them, Chuck Mountain, for a spin one evening on the public roads around Le Mans. Very rapidly the speedometer needle wound round the clock until they were doing around 175 mph – by now it was dark – and as they screamed along through the narrow roads, with the great engine thundering away behind them, McLaren called triumphantly, 'There, there – can you hear the misfire?'

'Hear the misfire!' replied Mountain. 'I can hear angels singing!'

Angels must surely have been at work when Craig Breedlove set his land speed record of 526 mph on Utah's Bonneville Salt Flats in October 1963, for during a test run the car swerved off the course, sheared off a telephone pole, careered wildly over a bank and ended up nose down in a canal. Miraculously, Breedlove escaped drowning and crawled out more or less intact. A year later he received a letter from the Mountain States Telephone and Telegraph Co. of Salt Lake City. It contained a demand for $200 for damage to telephone pole No. 4185 of the Salt Lake–Wendover line.

THE CAUTIOUS LOADER

Lord Warwick was out shooting on the bleak Cawdor Moors one wild and windy day, together with his faithful loader. He took aim and fired at a high bird which had come over right in front of him. He shot it; then, without a second's pause, swivelled round and aimed at another, which he missed.

'Almost as soon as I pressed the trigger,' he wrote, 'I received a tremendous blow on the side of my face that fairly knocked me over in the butt. My loader pulled me to my feet, and I realized that the bird I had shot at first, falling dead through the air while travelling at the rate of an express train, had struck me as it fell. Very dazed and a little angry I said to my loader, "Didn't you see that bird coming?" "Yes my Lord," was the unexpected reply, "I did see it coming. That is why I hid behind your Lordship."'

COWESLIP AND BLUE HEAVEN

The Duke of Edinburgh was racing his Flying Fifteen *Coweslip* with Uffa Fox during Cowes Week in 1962 when a series of near misses resulted in *Coweslip* going about too sharply, laying over and filling with water. In the process *Coweslip* fouled another Flying Fifteen, *Blue Heaven*, which was manned by T. Westbrook. Uffa Fox pointed out afterwards that he had told the Duke to go under the stern of *Blue Heaven*, but it was too late.

Such incidents are all part of sailing, so no doubt the Duke was not too despondent when the two repaired to Uffa's private quay at the bottom half of his garden in Cowes. Uffa was winching *Coweslip* out of the water with his private hoist – a rusty old piece of machinery – and the Duke was standing by, looking on.

Suddenly there was a crash, and down came *Coweslip*, out of 'blue heaven', inches from the Duke's head. No one was hurt.

THOMPSON'S CATCH

Neville Cardus gives some intriguing accounts of that literary cricketer, Sir John Squire. He describes a team of literary men and artists, such as Sir John might have assembled, to play against some sleepy Somerset village 'in a midsummer dream'. There is Arnold Bax the composer, his brother the author, Alec Waugh (though not *his* brother), the painter C. R. W. Nevinson, Hugh Walpole, and the musician William Murdoch. They travel down from London by train, alighting at Taunton. After these eminent figures have been playing seriously for an hour or two it is suddenly discovered that no one has been keeping the score. No one has been watching, for that matter, except for a solitary cow, so what can they do? There is a good deal of arguing with the captain of the Somerset village team, in which the

intelligentsia are forced to abandon their theoretical reconstruction of the score, which involves an allowance for the slowing effect of long grass in the outfield. Finally, everyone agrees to start all over again – though by this time Cardus is exhausted, and is replaced by Walpole, who after finding that he does not bowl too well with his right arm, finds he is better with his left. 'The result of the match,' writes Cardus, 'escapes my dream.'

The membership of Sir John's team varied in skill and talents from match to match. On another occasion one of the batsmen mishit a longhop and 'skied' the ball very high to mid-wicket. Of course, as usual, five or six fieldsmen all advanced with outstretched hands to make the catch. With rare presence of mind and true leadership, Sir John cried out: 'Thompson's catch! Leave it to Thompson!' Whereat each of the five or six fieldsmen retreated obediently – and the ball fell harmlessly to earth. Thompson was not playing that week.

THE SANDWICH TUNNY

Anglers on the harbour pier at Folkestone are not big-game fishermen. On one occasion however, shortly after the Second World War, they were so flooded out with tunny that the fishing had to stop. This memorable event occurred on 20th October 1946, and must have been a boon in the days of rationing. The only drawback from the sporting angle was that the tunny was actually dead. In fact it was already tinned – and crated. It had floated ashore from the freighter *Helena Mogeska*, which had broken up and beached a few miles away round the coast at Sandwich. A fishing contest had to be abandoned as the floating crates piled up round the pier.

The fishermen of Folkestone do seem to have had a run of peculiar catches at about this time. Scarcely a year later one of them, Charles Dalby, going down to check his shore lines on

Folkestone Warren beach one Friday morning, found that he had caught a fox. It had struggled before dying, he says, and he conjectures that it may have seized the bait when the line was lying on the sand at low tide.

CHU-CHU BANG-BANG

A game warden in Indiana in the winter of 1964 witnessed one of the most outrageous affronts to the pheasant ever perpetrated on either side of the Atlantic.

What alerted the warden first was the odd way the train kept backing up. He was looking at the train because it ran through his game preserve, and he noticed that it would run along as trains do for a space, then stop, then go into reverse and back up a hundred yards or so. There was just the engine and the guard's van, so it wasn't much of a train, but it was certainly behaving in an unorthodox way. Then the sound of a shotgun and the sight of a figure scurrying through the undergrowth suddenly made everything clear.

The warden turned on his walkie-talkie, called up the next station along the line, and when the train pulled in the sheriff was waiting. The evidence was lying in the caboose: three pheasants, two already dressed and one partly dressed, and a loaded shotgun. There are certain things a sportsman simply does not do when out shooting. In America the unwritten laws are slightly different, but still there are limits. The guard was charged with hunting without a licence, shooting in an unlawful manner and possession of a loaded uncased weapon. He has never been asked to any of the really top shoots again.

SAIL, MUSCLE AND POWER

Wind-surfing must be one of the most fiasco-prone sports ever invented. You are expected to stand on a slippery board which barely floats in the water, holding on to a pivoted sail with which you catch the wind. You don't. You fall off: again and again, and even when you are good you go on falling off at unexpected moments. The word fiasco is hardly adequate to describe the proceedings. But a true fiasco is something more than this. In a true fiasco a wind-surfer would be lifted by a waterspout, carried ahead of the competition and deposited just past the finishing line, only to be disqualified for having the number on his sail upside down.

An ancestor of the sport, or at least a variant on the theme, was surf boating, in which the board is propelled by a paddle. This was popular in the Lebanon in the 1960s, and competitions were held, many of which were won by the Lebanese Bahij Zuhaiki. In September 1964 Zuhaiki determined to try for a long-distance record by paddling his board across the Mediterranean from St George's Bay, Beirut to Cyprus, a distance of 110 nautical miles.

An escort boat was obviously essential, as the weather in the eastern Mediterranean has a habit of turning treacherous at short notice, so the 42-foot cruiser *Riana* was persuaded to stand in. The precaution appeared to be a wise one, for on the second evening the weather turned bad and the sea started to rise. Ten miles from their destination the *Riana* lost sight of Zuhaiki, still balanced on his board and paddling strongly as he crested the high waves. A few hours later, just 36 sleepless hours from the start, the champion beached his craft on Greco Bay, Famagusta, saying that he felt fine, but was worried about the *Riana*. An RAF search plane was sent out, and *Riana* was found 30 miles to the northeast of the island, wallowing helplessly on the rough sea with both engines out of action. She had to be towed in by a tug.

LOSING THEIR MAGIC

The Yellow Perils Football team of what was then Salisbury, Rhodesia lost all its trophies in 1956, despite hiring a witch doctor to improve its chances. A supporter later suggested that since they had only paid their witch doctor £10 his spells may not have been as potent as those of their opponents' witch doctor. But Bulawayo footballers professed scorn for the whole idea, emphasizing the scientific nature of the game, and hinting that this was just the sort of behaviour they would expect from Salisbury. In Bulawayo no one would ever be so superstitious. They went on to say that football matches, as a matter of cast iron certainty, were won or lost according to how well you played. It had nothing to do with how much you paid your witch doctor.

It was later disclosed by an official of the Salisbury and District Football Association that in 1954 and 1955, which were much better years for the club, 'not less than £20' had been paid. The problem however appeared to be that 'the 1956 executive did not believe in charms'.

Shirley Jackson wrote a highly successful book, *The Lottery*, dealing with witchcraft. She became obsessed with the idea that she too had abnormal powers, and when she became angry with her publisher, Alfred Knopf, in the unreasoning and groundless way that authors have, she decided to deal with him by occult means. Knopf at this time was skiing in Vermont, so Shirley Jackson made a wax model of the publisher and stuck a pin in one leg. Knopf broke the leg in three places.

ON THEIR KNEES

Little advantage is to be gained by any excessive display of religious emotion during a match. In 1967 during a soccer game in Bulgaria the referee got down on one knee and bowed his head in silence. Immediately the linesmen and the players of both teams – assuming that he was honouring some religious festival or local saint – followed his example. The spectators were puzzled, but a hush settled over the stadium for one scared minute. Then the referee, who had finished tying his shoelace, lifted his head.

Another kneeling player with genuinely religious motives was the Brazilian Isadore Irandir, goalkeeper of the Rio Prêto team. He always used to kneel in prayer at the goalmouth before a match. His side was playing Corinthians at Bahia Stadium when within three seconds of the starting whistle the ball was passed to Roberto Rivelino who scored instantly from the halfway line – before Irandir had time to get off his knees.

During the 1968 Rally of the Cedars in Lebanon Gerry Phillips was driving a Volvo, with the assistance of two Lebanese navigators. The navigators were always losing the way, so Phillips had to drive very fast to make up lost time, turning at the hairpin bends of the escarpment roads by means of nicely judged four-wheel skids. One navigator was in the front of the car, begging Phillips to remember that he had eight children. The other was on his knees in the back, praying.

'Please, Mr Phillips', he implored, 'do not fall over the edge, or we'll fall into Israel.'

MIXED SPORTS

The American Amateur Athletic Union indoor championships of February 1974 demonstrate how important it is to keep one sport separate from another. No wonder oarsmen are so sensitive about being confused with canoeists, or tennis players with table-tennis players – or real tennis players with either.

The long jumper at this event – Olympic gold medallist Randy Williams – was jogging round the track to warm up when he stumbled on a stone, fell down and sprained his ankle. Shortly after this, during the women's sprint, a vaulter knocked a cross bar into a track just in time to trip up the leading runner, Carmen Brown of the Atoms Track Club. And as a pole vaulter was just taking off the starter of the men's relay, who was standing a few feet away, fired his pistol. The vaulter, poor chap, slithered down his pole and collapsed in a heap.

MOOSE HOOTS

The secret of attracting moose, as American hunters well know, is to make exactly the right noise at them. The animals are easily persuaded that anything which hoots in a moose-like way is a potential mate. On occasion, they have even mistaken the whistle of a diesel locomotive for the cry of one of their kind, and have been lured to their death on the railway lines.

In euphoniously named Flin Flon, Manitoba one afternoon in the autumn of 1961, two moose hunters were prowling the bush, giving out their best grunting hoots. Each got closer and closer to his prey, stalking stealthily through the bush: then, with a final triumphant hoot the hunters sprang round the trunk of a big spruce – to confront each other.

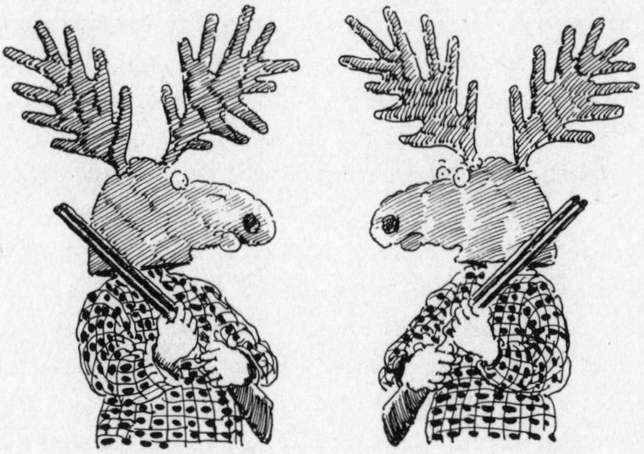

HEADLINES

THE END OF THE WORLD read the headline in the *Scottish Daily Express* when Scotland drew 1–1 with outsiders Iran in the World Cup Finals in 1978. Sports-writers do exaggerate. When the Irish rugby international player Tony O'Reilly returned after leaving the game for a spell as an executive for the Heinz Corporation in the United States, and did not live up to expectations, an unkind editor headed the account of the match HEINZ MEANZ HAZ BEENZ.

The Crystal Palace club has also provided writers with an opportunity for ingenious headlines – particularly as two of the players for the club were named Burns and Queen. Headlines on this theme have included QUEEN IN BRAWL AT PALACE and PALACE FIDDLE WHILE BURNS ROAMED.

The following story, however, told to me by the fisheries correspondent of a major London newspaper, who happened to be in Norway covering a story about a fishing dispute, demonstrates how much can be compressed into a few short words. After reporting on the dispute, the writer attended a local rugby match. It was between a male and a female team, and the women, the 'Fjord Nymphs', were widely fancied to win, since celebrations the night before in honour of the men's team, who had just beaten an Oslo side, had left them in a debilitated state.

As predicted, the women played a vigorous game and managed to beat the men, who took their defeat with a rather bad grace. To restore friendly relations the women that evening invited them to a dance at the village hall. This enraged the men still further, and they went on the rampage.

'All we did was ask them for a quick waltz,' said the captain of the Fjord Nymphs sadly.

The fisheries correspondent thought the affair sufficiently curious to warrant sending the story in to the sports desk of his newspaper in Fleet Street. It was published the following day under the following headline: FJORD NYMPHS XV BEG QUICK WALTZ.

What is so special about that? It happens to be the only sentence ever devised in the English language which contains every letter of the alphabet once, and once only.

NAMES

The Boston Red Sox baseball pitcher Bill Monbouquette, who used to appear regularly at Yankee Stadium, had a characteristic way of cupping his groin at the jockstrap at the end of a delivery, giving it a little heft, as if rearranging what was within. The poet Marianne Moore noticed him doing this when she was taken to a match and commented on the appealing insouciance of the gesture, remarking that he should not be told. Taking out her notebook, she wrote his name down, murmuring, 'My little bouquet.'

There are some names which are a positive temptation to commentators, such as those of two baseball umpires in Florida – Albine Batt and John Ball, while Coatesville High of Coatesville, Pennsylvania boasted until recently a pole vaulter named Robert Jump and a female sprinter called Sonia Runner.

After a test match at the Oval against the West Indies, the commentator Brian Johnston received a letter from a Miss Mainpiece, reprimanding him for loose language on the air. At the beginning of an over bowled by the West Indian fast bowler Michael Holding to Peter Willey, Johnston apparently stated, in all innocence, 'The bowler's Holding, the batsman's Willey.'

It is a pleasant idea for sports enthusiasts to name their children after their heroes, but I do feel that Brian and Susan Brown of Park Road, Wrottesley, Wolverhampton, were going too far when in April 1974 they named their two-month-old daughter after 25 heavyweight boxers: Maria Sullivan Corbett Fitzsimmons Jeffries Hart Burns Johnson Willard Dempsey Tunney Schmeling Sharkey Carnera Baer Braddock Louis Charles Walcott Marciano Patterson Johansson Liston Clay Frazier Foreman Brown.

12

You Can't Always Win

Where it is impossible to blame anyone or anything else for a sporting fiasco, one has to bear in mind that in any competitive game there must be a winner and a loser (unless the match is a draw, which is itself a fiasco). No matter how much of a superstar you are, you have to remember this simple law of life: you can't always win.

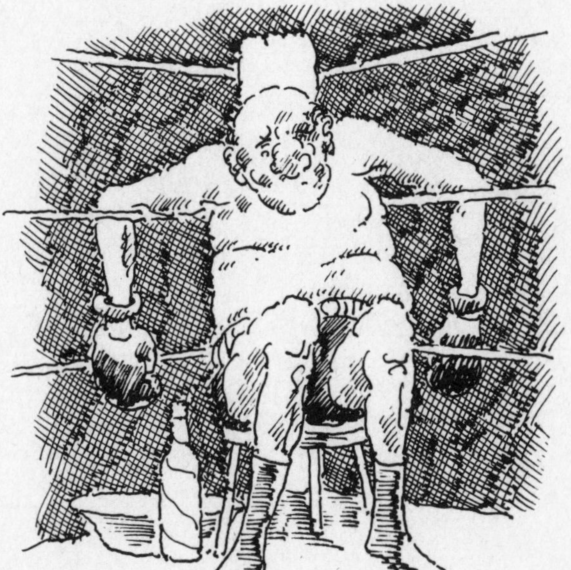

DISASTERS HAPPEN IN SIXES

The worst moment in the sporting life of the jockey and writer Lord Oaksey happened at Cheltenham. The annoying thing was that he was about to win. He was about a fence in front, with only one other horse left behind him, when he was suddenly overwhelmed by the (mistaken) conviction that he had gone the wrong way. He pulled up, turned round, and shouted an unnecessary warning to his only surviving rival – who ignored it and went on to win. The crowd booed, the stewards fined him £25, he ricked his back and went off home in low spirits, to nurse the back in a hot bath.

As he was running the bath the telephone rang. It was a commiserating friend. What an awful business . . . How could it have happened . . . and so on. It took some explaining.

Finally Lord Oaksey put the telephone down and hobbled back to the bathroom – where the tap was still running and the floor was six inches deep in hot water.

TOTAL FRUSTRATION

How many of us have placed a bet that 'almost won'. Or worse still, an accumulator bet that went part of the way and then fizzled out just when enormous winnings appeared within reach.

Perhaps one of the most frustrating bets ever was placed by Christopher Hill, a management consultant and the inventor of the betting system named 'Computerform'.

The fatal day was a Friday, the last in May 1968, and Mr Hill's betting card was as follows:

Race No.	1	2	3	4	5	6
Win	1	1	2	2	1	1
Second	2	6		3	2	4
Third						9
Fourth						15

By some miraculous combination of luck, judgement and electronics every one of these bets was correct, and Mr Hull approached the Tote window with a confident feeling that for a stake of £16 he was about to collect the jackpot – £16,222.

To his astonishment he was met with a blank refusal. It was against the regulations, he was told. What regulations, for goodness sake? Well, it was all to do with the second horse in the first race. No. 2 was a non-starter, so the bet on No. 2 to place second was wrong. Hull's reply to this piece of news was that it was no news at all, because he had watched the Epsom Stakes, and was fully aware that No. 2 had withdrawn, but his bet was still valid, because where there is a non-starter the bet goes on the favourite. It so happened that the favourite was Folle Russe who came second, so could he please have his cheque?

He could not. The reason, it was explained, was that Folle Russe was not the favourite but the *joint* favourite, joint favourite with the winner of the race, which he had correctly predicted – Margera (No. 1). And when there is a joint favourite the bet goes on whichever of the two horses has the lower number. Now, one is a lower number than three, it will be agreed. Therefore his bet for the second place, as well as the first, was Margera – or if he preferred it that way, his second bet was a wasted bet. No jackpot for Mr Hull.

PRINCELY REBUKE

It might be thought that Queen Elizabeth II's heir would be allowed to enjoy his moments of leisure and sport with rather fewer incidental irritations than most of his future subjects, but such is by no means the case.

In July 1973 the Prince of Wales was in Nassau for the Bahamas' Independence Day Celebrations. Two days before Independence Day a polo match was arranged, which must have seemed an enjoyable respite from the more formal receptions which filled the Prince's tour. Prince Charles is normally a confident performer, and if he does occasionally fall off his horse, well, so do all polo players. But this time he was becoming distinctly flustered. It was not so much the brilliance of his opponents, who were from a neighbouring island; nor was it his horse: he was used to handling all sorts and conditions of animal. The weather was faultless, and there was not a hint of an earthquake or a volcanic eruption. The only fly in the ointment was this infuriating voice on the loudspeaker.

'And coming up on the inside of the field now is that well-known figure Prince Whatsisname – ' The commentator was an American player and this was typical of the way he referred to the Prince. He was having a lot of fun.

'Here comes the Prince again – Prince Philip I think it is: oh, look, I think he's going to fall off,' and so on. The 'Philip' joke repeated at least twice.

The Royal blood finally boiled over when Prince Charles missed a difficult pass.

'Great shot, Prince!' said the irrepressible voice.

Prince Charles dismounted, went over to the commentator's box and delivered a few doubtless well-chosen words. The irrepressible voice was successfully repressed. The commentary ceased immediately.

THE TRIUMPHANT HURDLER

The 1974 Commonwealth Olympic Games at Christchurch, New Zealand were drawing to a close. The 400 metres hurdles had been won triumphantly by Alan Pascoe. The crowd were cheering. Pascoe thought he would reward them with a lap of honour. Acknowledging their accolade with a nonchalant wave over his shoulder, he set off for the first hurdle. (In fact it was the last hurdle since he was at the end of the course.) He took a great leap at it . . . and knocked it down. Raising his hands in mock horror and pausing to set it upright again, he set off once more. This time he crashed right through it.

GREAT LOSERS

To some people, sport comes naturally. These are the heroes of sport, the superstars. Others find the going harder.

For example, in 1961 Edward Simmonds, the 12-year-old goalkeeper of Nottingham Workshop Sea Cadets' soccer team, established a record for letting in the largest number of goals in consecutive matches. Edward, who was at the time only 4 feet 10 inches tall – in itself a disadvantage for a goalkeeper – was not deterred by a 25–1 defeat in his first game of the series, as his side went on to lose 33–0, 21–0, 28–0, 34–0 and 24–0. From this point on a marked improvement took place: in their following match the Cadets scored a goal – though Edward let in 25. Finally, thanks to his accumulated experience, Edward managed to keep the other side's score, in the last match of the series, to a mere 14 goals, though this time the Cadets' score was zero again. This makes a total of 204 goals let in during eight games.

Like all sporting achievements, Edward Simmonds's was eventually eclipsed. Other milestones along the road included a famous match between the Edinburgh Dynamos ladies' team and Lochend Thistle, in which the women from Thistle lost 44–1. Perhaps the crowning effort in this area was the Japanese college soccer game in which Osaka Seikei Women's Junior College beat Konan Women's Junior College by 221 goals to zero, on 16th July 1981. Quite how this feat was performed in the available time is hard to grasp, but no doubt Japanese technology was responsible.

Another triumphant score was achieved in Yugoslavia, where there is a somewhat heated rivalry between natives of Serbia, Macedonia and Albania. The Ilenden Football Club, anxious to secure promotion to the first division in 1979, managed, through what can only be described as collusion, to beat Mladost by 134 goals to one.

At a somewhat higher level was the extraordinary defeat of the English World Cup team in Brazil in 1950. This was no freak high score – quite the reverse. It was the worst defeat the English side has ever received, for they were playing against the US team, who were semi-amateur, and were hardly thought of as serious contenders for the Cup. When news of the 1–0 defeat reached Fleet Street they thought it was a 10–0 victory! It was assumed there must be an error in the cable. Sir Alf Ramsey, to the question 'Were you playing for the English team in the 1950 World Cup match in Brazil?' once replied, 'Yes, I was the only one who was.'

In Rugby football a number international matches stand out, including Wales's victory over Japan by 82–6 in 1975, and the defeat of Scotland by South Africa 44–0 at Murrayfield in 1951.

In cricket of course scores are numerically larger, and scores have, on rare occasions, reached the thousands. But possibly the most decisive defeat of all time occurred at Pakistan Railways' match against Dera Ismail Khan in December 1964. After amassing a total of 910 for six declared, the railwaymen went on to dismiss their opponents for 32 runs.

RATTLING IVANOV

The Australian Olympic oarsman Stewart 'Sam' Mackenzie has rowed many times against the Russian Vyacheslav Ivanov, who three times won the Olympic gold medal in the single sculls. But

Mackenzie, who won a Silver in the 1956 Ballarat Regatta on Lake Wendouree, was never beaten by Ivanov at Henley. There is a difference in the lengths of the two courses which in part explains Ivanov's disadvantage, for he was trained very hard for the Olympic course, whereas Mackenzie excelled at the longer distance.

Mackenzie, a somewhat larger-than-life figure, was determined to rattle Ivanov when he visited Henley for the Diamond Sculls the year after Ivanov's victory at Lake Wendouree. Shortly after the start of the race he pulled out of his lane into the Russian's, and remained less than a length behind him, timing his strokes to be exactly out of step. As Ivanov swung his oars forward for the start of a stroke, Mackenzie would surge ahead, while on Ivanov's power stroke Mackenzie's oars would be reaching forward towards the Russian. Thus the bow of Mackenzie's boat thrust forward and fell back in such a way as to cause his opponent the maximum upset to his rhythm.

After rowing on for some distance, Mackenzie sensed that Ivanov was getting tired, because he could hear the sound of the oars 'washing out' as his stroke grew clumsier and he started to throw up spray. This was Mackenzie's signal to put on a tremendous spurt, taking him past his by now demoralized opponent, who, realizing that he was beaten, slackened his pace. Mackenzie sculled on strongly to the finish, lengths ahead.

After passing the finishing line the Australian turned his skiff and sculled back down to the enclosure, spun round, and deliberately lost one oar under the floating boom marker. At this point Ivanov arrived on the scene. Seeing the struggling oarsman and the excited crowd, hope suddenly revived, and he summoned up his last reserves of energy. It was obvious that Mackenzie would never get his oar back in time to finish, and as he triumphantly sped over the finishing line he waved at the Australian, making a 'V' sign with his fingers. But there was something about the nervous titter that went up from the onlookers, and the way Mackenzie was slumped over his one remaining oar shaking convulsively with suppressed laughter... Then Ivanov caught the judge's embarrassed expression and the awful truth came home to him.

SHORTER MARATHON

The English marathon runner Dr Ron Hill remembers 10th September 1972 as a muggy, overcast day in Munich. He was wearing a pair of specially designed silver sun-reflecting running shorts, but as there was no sun to reflect they contributed nothing to his performance. Indeed they may have been a psychological disadvantage for that very reason, though most athletes would be proud to have achieved sixth place in an Olympic marathon.

A vast, expectant crowd awaited the arrival of the first runner in the stadium. Gigantic electronic scoreboards kept spectators and journalists up-to-the-minute with the positions of all the major competitors. The American runner Frank Shorter was in the lead, well ahead of Karel Lismont in second place and the Ethiopian Mamo Wolde in third. Any minute now Shorter would be coming into view.

Suddenly an enormous roar went up as a slim, curly-haired figure in yellow shorts, looking superbly fresh, came pounding into the stadium. Round the great track he ran, to the ecstatic applause of the crowd. Hats flew off, whistles blew, programmes fluttered from the stands. The air was filled with cheering.

The only drawback to this supreme Olympic accolade was that the runner was not Frank Shorter. No, he was a certain Norbert Sudhaus, a 22-year-old German student who had joined the race just outside the stadium. Well might he look fresh, for he had run no more than a few hundred metres. Behind him, second to enter the stadium, having run the regulation 42,195 metres, was the real Frank Shorter. How many people in the crowd identified the number 1014 on his vest? To judge from the sparse applause that greeted the true winner nearly everyone had been taken in – until the insouciant runner in the yellow shorts was led off by security officials.

THE GREATEST TEE IN THE WORLD

Those little plastic spigots golfers use to raise the ball off the ground have a curiously satisfying shape, broadening out to a cup at one end, tapering to a point at the other. Invert one so that it stands on the cup, magnify it about ten thousand times, square it off a bit, and what have you got? The Eiffel Tower.

When Arnold Palmer thought up the idea of teeing off from the Eiffel Tower he was expressing a wish that must be near to the heart of every golfer – simply to hit a ball further than anyone ever has before. Palmer made two attempts at fulfilling this impossible dream. The first time, in October 1976, having got the police to close the Champ de Mars to traffic, he ascended the 377 feet to the second stage of the tower only to find a stiff breeze blowing into his face from the direction of the Ecole Militaire. Nevertheless he teed up his ball and drove off, achieving 276 yards with his best shot.

Hoping to do better, he tried again in October of the following year. Rising early, the pink-shirted Palmer reached his 377-foot-high teeing-off point at 8.30 am. It was a fine and brilliant morning, perfect for golf, and all Paris lay at his feet, shimmering in the sunlight – 'quite an eyeful', as a reporter at the scene remarked. Palmer hit three balls – 323 yards, 363 yards and a

magnificent 402 yards. The last would count as one of the longest golf drives in history if Palmer hadn't hooked the ball. It curved off sideways towards Les Invalides, described a perfect arc through the bright air, and landed with an audible ping on the roof of a passing bus.

ACKNOWLEDGEMENTS

I am extremely grateful to the following people, without whom this book could not have been written: Lord Aberdare; Ted Avory; Pat Besford, past President of the British Sports Writers Association; Mike Carlson; Major T. Cooper, Curator, the Wimbledon Lawn Tennis Museum; Mike da Costa; Chris Dodd; Colin Dryden; Polly Drysdale; Colin Elsey and Stuart Fraser of Colour Sport Ltd; Commander Gerald Forsberg OBE; John Goodbody; Stephen Green, Curator of Lord's Cricket Ground Museum and Library; Sir Hugh Greene; Colin Hart; David Hunn; Vani Ivanovic; Brian Johnston; Chris Lander; Roy McKelvie; Norris McWhirter; John Moynihan; Morley Myers; Lt.-Col. Tom Nickalls; Douglas Nye; Lord Oaksey; Gerry Phillips; Mrs Murlo Primrose; Jim Railton; Tony Reay; John Rodda; Max Robertson; John Young; Count Adam Zamoyski. Thanks are also due to Patricia Moynagh for her imaginative and painstaking research; and to the mongrel dog which bit me on the way back from a lamentably brief though memorable meeting with John Arlott in Alderney, thereby adding tremendous impetus to my researches into the odder aspects of sport.

Grateful acknowledgements are due to the following publishers and authors: *The Times*; *Sports Illustrated*; Neville Cardus, *Autobiography* (Collins, London 1947); Chris Dodd, *Henley Royal Regatta* (Stanley Paul/Hutchinson, London 1981); Brendan Gill, *Here at the New Yorker* (*New Yorker*, New York 1975); David Guiney, *The Dunlop Book of the Olympic Games* (Lavenham Press 1972); Brian Johnston, *Rain Stops Play* (W. H. Allen, London 1979); Lord Killanin and John Rodda, *The Olympic Games* (Barrie & Jenkins, London 1975); the Estate of the late Sonia Brownell Orwell and Martin Secker & Warburg Ltd; George Plimpton, *Shadow Box* (Berkley, New York 1977); Ted Ray, *Golf: My Slice of Life* (W. H. Allen, London 1972); Jonathan Ruffer, *The Big Shots* (Debretts, London 1979); Anthony Smith, *The Dangerous Sort* (Allen & Unwin, London 1970).

INDEX